Re-Creative

Re-Creative

50 projects for turning found items into contemporary design

Steve Dodds

HOME

A HOME BOOK

Published by the Penguin Group

Penguin Group (USA) Inc.

375 Hudson Street, New York, New York 10014, USA

This edition is published by Penguin in the following
territories: USA. All other rights held by Elwin Street.

Other Penguin offices worldwide:

Penguin Group (Canada), 90 Eglinton Avenue East, Suite 700, Toronto,
Ontario M4P 2Y3, Canada
(a division of Pearson Penguin Canada Inc.)
Penguin Books Ltd., 80 Strand, London WC2R 0RL, England
Penguin Group Ireland, 25 St. Stephen's Green, Dublin 2, Ireland
(a division of Penguin Books Ltd.)
Penguin Group (Australia), 250 Camberwell Road, Camberwell, Victoria
3124, Australia
(a division of Pearson Australia Group Pty. Ltd.)
Penguin Books India Pvt. Ltd., 11 Community Centre, Panchsheel Park,
New Delhi—110 017, India
Penguin Group (NZ), Cnr. Airborne and Rosedale Roads, Albany,
Auckland 1310, New Zealand
(a division of Pearson New Zealand Ltd.)
Penguin Books (South Africa) (Pty.) Ltd., 24 Sturdee Avenue, Rosebank,
Johannesburg 2196, South Africa
Penguin Books Ltd., Registered Offices: 80 Strand, London
WC2R 0RL, England

Copyright © 2006 by Elwin Street

Conceived and produced by Elwin Street Limited
144 Liverpool Road, London N1 1LA
www.elwinstreet.com

Design: Louise Leffler
Photography: Paul Bricknell and Maya Barkai
Extra projects supplied by Kanchana Arni for pages 34, 62, 68–70, 102,
104–6, 107, 120, 122–4, 125, and 128–9.

HOME is a registered trademark of Penguin Group (USA) Inc. The
"Home" design is a trademark belonging to Penguin Group (USA) Inc.
First edition: December 2006
Library of Congress Cataloging-in-Publication Data

Dodds, Steve.
  Re-creative : 50 projects for turning found items into contemporary
  design / Steve Dodds.
    p. cm.
  Includes index.
  ISBN 1-55788-509-5
  1. Handicraft. 2. Recycling (Waste, etc.) 3. House furnishings. I. Title.
  TT157.D634 2006
  745.5-dc22
                              2006023696

Printed in China

10 9 8 7 6 5 4 3 2 1

Most Home Books are available at special quantity discounts for bulk
purchases for sales promotions, premiums, fund-raising, or educational
use. Special books, or book excerpts, can also be created to fit specific
needs. For details, write: Special Markets, The Berkley Publishing
Group, 375 Hudson Street, New York, New York 10014.

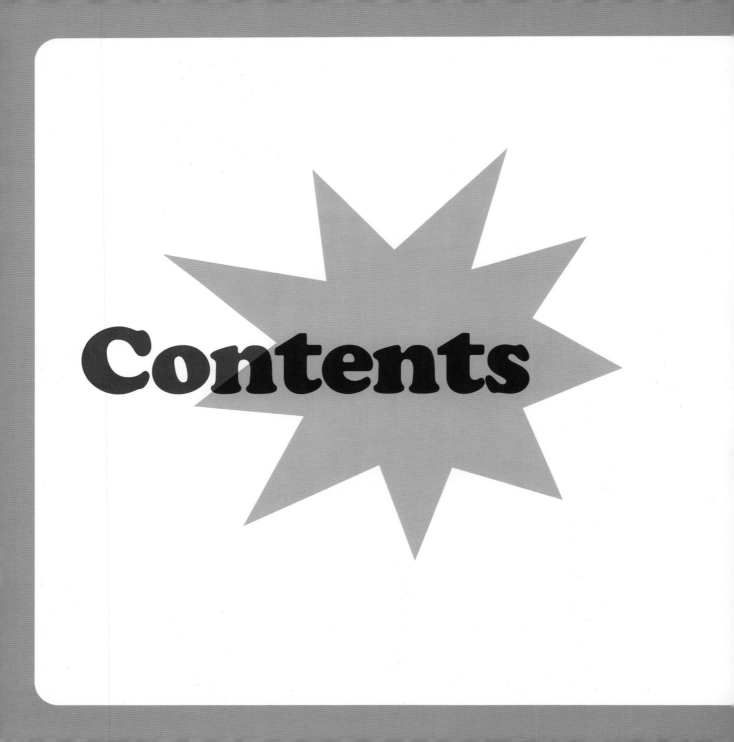

Contents

Introduction

Re-creation: the act of making anew
Recreation: activity done for enjoyment

Without leaving the mall, you can buy pre-faded T-shirts with "vintage" graphics, distressed furniture with factory-applied patina, or home accessories that mimic the style of decades ago. Each gives the appearance of having a history and a soul. In reality, it's just the same mass-produced stuff that everyone else is buying.

Making something for yourself is not only enjoyable in its own right, but gives you the satisfaction of having an item that is unique. Reusing found or salvaged items conserves materials, is cost-effective, and imbues your finished product with a story much more worth retelling than "I bought it at Crate and Barrel."

The fifty projects covered in the following pages are the material equivalent of a musical remix. They take the found and the cast-off, add to them, and throw the sum into a new context for your enjoyment. Reused and re-purposed materials are the heart of the book, and our goal is to adapt materials in a simple way—to make things that function well, are pleasing to the eye, well-crafted, and pleasurable to have around.

In Getting Started (pages 10–23), you'll find background info on design plus ideas for coming up with your own projects and sourcing materials. The rest of the book is dedicated to ready-to-make projects, which include tools, techniques, and everything you need to know to get re-creative in your own home. In three categories: Furniture, Accessories, and Fabric, there's something for every object. From making a functional bedside table out of cardboard (page 65) to a lampshade from your train tickets (page 52), this book is an inspiration for turning common cast-offs into cool designs.

Getting Started

Creating a new project is a process of balancing a series of competing and interrelated decisions and requirements. To make things more challenging, when you start, you never have all the information you need to solve the problem at hand. Sometimes you'll begin with a material and figure out something to do with it, other times you'll have a need and have to come up with something to fulfill it.

Sound daunting? It's not really. By the time you're done, you'll know what it is that you want to make. You'll have an idea of what you want it to look like and what size it should be. You'll have decided what the thing will be made from and how it will be assembled. You'll figure these things out based on experience, dumb luck, and trial and error. (Okay, mostly trial and error.)

Basically, the design process takes a little bit of research, and then some experimenting and playing around until you get a result that seems right. This is not so bad. (It's quite fun actually.)

It's clear that you have some interest in projects that are appealing due to their simplicity rather than their heavily applied decoration, otherwise you'd have bought "40 Projects for Your Victorian Drawing Room," or something like that. The desire for simple, quality craftsmanship is far from an original concept, so let's first take a quick look at what has driven people in the past to create designs in this vein. A knowledge of what others have done helps channel your ideas as you work through a design. We'll then dive into some ways that materials can be reused by your average Jane and Joe and get into specifics about what to look for and where to find it.

The re-creative design process takes a little bit of research and then some experimenting and playing around until you get a result that seems right.

An Inspiration to Careful Craftsmanship

Simple, utilitarian items were the norm for most people throughout history. They were generally a means to an end and nothing more. Built to do the job, but not for appearance. Higher levels of craftsmanship were reserved for items that served a decorative need as well as a functional one. A group called the Shakers mixed this up a bit.

The desire for simple, quality craftsmanship is far from an original concept. A knowledge of what others have done helps channel your ideas as you work through a design.

The Shakers (or "The Society of United Believers" as they were officially known) were a religious group that flourished in the north-eastern United States in the mid-1800s. People in this sect sought to live simply and communally, separate from the world at large, as an expression of their faith. Church doctrine prescribed celibacy, plainness in dress, speech and behavior, simplicity, thrift, and orderliness. Similarly, worldly fanciness, ornament, and superfluous possessions were forbidden.

As the sect developed, Shaker settlements farmed their own land and started producing a variety of goods, first for their own use and later for sale to generate income. The way they made their products reflected the simplicity with which they conducted their lives.

Their approach to work was of key importance to the quality of the items they made. Work was considered a noble act and was to be undertaken efficiently, skillfully, and to the best of one's ability, both for the benefit of the group and as a personal act of devotion. Craftsmanship was seen not just as desirable in itself, but as a testament of the maker's faith.

Above The Eames rocker, said to be the most significant furniture design of the twentieth century.

The resulting form of Shaker products was based on the item's function, the need for durability, and the materials used. Just as an individual in the sect focused his or her existence on worship, the products he or she made were simply and solely devoted to the purposes they served. The minimum amount of material was used to make an item sturdy and sound. Connections and detailing took into account any peculiar qualities of the materials used, for example, seasonal expansion and contraction of wood.

So here we have a model for thoughtfully creating products using humble materials, built with careful craftsmanship, to create something functional and meaningful.

Modern Design

The clean and simple lines of modern design were borne out of a reaction against unnecessary ornament and with a concern for function and efficiency in fabrication. While faith was the driving force in the Shakers' culture, early in the twentieth century new industries, a rapidly changing society, and hope for the future spurred communities of artists, designers, and architects into action.

In the first half of the century, the market's desire for profit and the shortages and urgencies of the two World Wars created a demand for strong and efficient products that spurred waves of innovation in materials and fabrication processes. Science was making it possible for products and devices that were merely fantasy a generation before to become reality.

However, many of the items that were being manufactured still mimicked the products that for centuries had been hand-produced.

Forcing new materials and methods to create something that looked "old" seemed counterintuitive to some people. Instead, they started to explore what could be achieved with the newly available materials and methods to take greater advantage of their strengths.

What they came up with were products that served their functions, but were more true to how they were made and, just like Shaker products, were minimal, finely crafted, and appealing.

The lesson here is experimentation. You can maintain values and goals for a project, while expressing it in a new or different way, based on the resources available to you (including materials, skills, and money).

We've looked at two different contexts for creation here and found some commonalities between them. Your projects may not end up looking Shaker-style or "Classic Modern," for that matter, but the values embodied in both schools of thought and the ways they were put into action are worth keeping in mind and using as inspiration.

Above This is a combination of a bent-plywood seat that was bought without legs from IKEA's "scratch and dent" department, and the rocker base from an Eames chair found *sans* seat in the Classifieds a few days later. It cost $75 altogether, but that's inexpensive compared to the alternatives available.

Junk and How to Use It

All around the world people have reused and reworked old things into new to meet the pressures of economy and necessity. Things were salvaged not because they added a certain *je ne sais quoi* to the user's home, but because the materials had a quality that could be incorporated into something else, and a value that was too good to be discarded.

Many of us may have been lucky enough not to have to live that way, but making the most of what we have and minimizing the amount that is discarded is a good way to protect our environment and our wallets.

This is one of the main differences between this book and other project books. For the most part, you won't need to run to the store to buy the materials listed. Some you'll need to acquire and accumulate and others you'll have to go hunting for. Trash is just about the only resource we're not depleting.

There are three ways to source supplies: things come to you, you stumble across something too cool to pass up, or you hunt it down.

Sourcing Recycled Materials

Before you can start to gather your materials, it usually helps to have at least a rough idea of what you'll need, although often it makes sense to acquire some things before you even have a project in mind. There are basically three ways to go about sourcing your supplies: things come to you, you stumble across something that is just too cool to pass up, or you hunt it down.

THINGS COME TO YOU

These are the sorts of things you accumulate with little effort, and include containers and packaging that you might otherwise routinely throw away. Set up a place to store them until you reach the critical mass of items needed for your project.

TOO COOL TO PASS UP

Sometimes an item catches your eye that you're sure you can do something interesting with, although what that is precisely doesn't quite spring to mind. It's a good idea to go with the hunch and pick it up. Just don't get too carried away with this or your house will end up looking like the set of *Sanford and Son*.

Because you never know what you'll come upon, it's helpful to carry a pocketknife or multi-tool with built-in screwdriver bits and pliers to enable you to strip parts off things you see set out for the trash. Sure, your pockets might be heavier, but you're being all re-creative now and it's worth it.

HUNT IT DOWN

Garage sales and flea markets are a source of unique finds, and they are also good places to find tools. Online classifieds are also a source of odd found objects. Photos often accompany the ads, so it's like wandering through a flea market from the comfort of your own desk.

Sometimes more detective work is needed. Waste generated by local businesses is a great resource. For our purposes, businesses fall into two categories. First, there are those that consistently discard the same manufactured, post-consumer items (such as carpet stores, which get rid of cardboard tubes, or a pizza place that regularly discards empty sauce jars).

The Yellow Pages are your best friend since they give an idea of where to start looking. For instance, approach appliance stores for big sheets of heavy cardboard (refrigerator boxes). Contacting a business by phone first saves you having to run around town and you may be able to talk them into holding onto some items for you or find out when things may become available.

Then there are those businesses that generate scraps and off-cuts during their fabrication process. These are especially useful if you don't need a large amount or can be flexible about size and color, etc. For example, lumberyards often have scrap bins containing pieces with defects or that are too short to store in the racks. Fabrication shops and material suppliers that work with plastics, stone, sheet metal, and upholstery also often have scrap bins.

Remember, when you're approaching a business, you're asking them to do you a favor and you should try to inconvenience them as little as possible. You need to have a good idea of what and how much of the item you'll need. Also, you may not be able to get exactly what you want, so you need to have an understanding of your project to be able to make some decisions on the fly and determine whether you can make do with the materials that are offered.

More Tips for Getting Started

✓ Plan ahead and consider if you need any tools to disassemble a scrounged item or cut it to size. Have an idea of how you'll get it home and take whatever is necessary to do so: a heavy bag, tape, rope, vehicle, your brother-in-law? Once you've got what you came for, make sure that anything you choose not to take is left neatly. Aside from just being nice, this makes it more likely that you'd be welcomed back in the future. This goes for things you pick apart on the curb, too. You don't want to make more work for the trash collectors or leave a mess someone else is going to have to clean up.

✓ When in doubt, make sure an item is free before carting it off. It sounds obvious, but sometimes a rush of creative juices to the brain can fog your commonsense.

✗ Until they've reached the end of their useful lives, avoid using things such as beer kegs, water jugs, and milk crates, which are meant to be returned and reused for their intended purpose. If you take one out of circulation, another one has to be made to take its place.

✗ Don't butcher something that has value as an antique or an historical artifact. For instance, if you're going to melt a vinyl record to make a bowl out of it, don't use a rare Charlie Parker import. Find something truly awful to sacrifice. (In fact, the world may even be a better place with one less Air Supply album in it.)

✓ If you're designing a project, try to build it so that when its life is over, it too can be reused or recycled.

✓ If using new materials, try to use those that contain recycled content and/or are recyclable. Use lumber that has been harvested from sustainable sources.

Consider your recycling ethics. Don't take a milk crate out of circulation until it's at the end of its natural life. If designing a project, try to build it so that it too can be reused or recycled.

Some Materials to Steer Clear Of

Generally it's a matter of commonsense, but sometimes it is worth being wary. Avoid containers that have held chemicals or liquids used in industry, which could pose a health hazard around the house. They are not something you want to introduce into your living space. Leftover cleaners, paints, and solvents have special disposal requirements and should not be mixed in with regular trash, but it pays to be careful. Similarly, be sure of the history of any materials that will be used around food or children.

Another caution is on electronic waste. Computers and electronics are chock-full of unpleasant heavy metals that have been associated with health risks. A computer monitor contains lead, along with a dash of mercury, cadmium, and barium. Chips and processors contain other chemicals. Capacitors may hold a residual charge long after the machine was last powered down and this means it is possible to get zapped. It's advisable to use only the cases, chassis, and miscellaneous nuts and bolts you can strip from CPUs, unless you're an electronics whiz.

If you are going to scrounge something from the trash, look things over before moving or messing with it. It's in the trash for a reason and may have sharp or broken parts.

And don't climb into dumpsters. Seriously.

Designing with Recycled Items

Ideally, you want your finished project to have the appearance and level of finish that will rival (dare we say, surpass) a store-bought item. With a limited range of recycled materials at your disposal, you may be at a disadvantage, but there are a few strategies to use that will add a quality of finish and interest to disguise this fact.

CREATE INTEREST BY USING UNORTHODOX MATERIALS

Examples would be using magazines or found art to make cards and envelopes; or making simple purses or knapsacks out of vinyl billboard material. The eye is attracted to these familiar items by the materials from which they are made. (See License Plate Box, page 26, for an example.)

USE AN OBJECT REPETITIVELY

The ordered presentation of one type of object over and over again makes an impact. Take advantage of order and regularity by using multiples of an object in a composition. Items that you purchase and discard daily are prime candidates for this purpose (see Metrocard Lampshade, page 52).

"CELEBRATE" A FOUND OBJECT

Present an item so that it is the focus of attention; this is most effective if it contrasts with its surroundings. A beat-up farm table in the corner of a barn is just that, but put it in a stark white New York City loft, and you perceive it entirely differently. A shell or tiny piece of driftwood goes unnoticed on a beach, but string it on a necklace, and it is displayed and appreciated. The presentation depends on the piece being incongruous with its surroundings and the effect can be diminished if the item is overshadowed. Any additions should be spare and minimal (see Scrap Stone Candleholder, page 32).

Of course, it goes without saying that it's a bad idea to scrounge and pilfer natural resources from the great outdoors. This is not what we mean by "reuse." Gather objects that have been discarded and then you are genuinely (and ethically) turning trash into treasure.

ALLOW THE OBJECTS TO BLEND SEAMLESSLY INTO A
NEW COMPOSITION

My favorite projects in this book are those with an interesting function that just "happen" to be made from reclaimed materials. It's as if they have a past life that only close inspection can reveal, and the fact that the project's parts are recycled takes a backseat to the new design (see Computer Case Table, page 47, for example).

USE UNUSUAL ACCESSORIES
Browse around the hardware store for interesting fasteners, handles, latches, and light bulbs. Screws that use a square drive or have recesses for an Allen wrench offer more of a finished look, as do oval head screws with trim washers. Position exposed fasteners evenly and consistently.

MIX CHEAP AND HIGH DESIGN
Humble materials have an appeal in their own right. Cardboard tubes, for example, take on a velvety texture when lightly sanded. But everything you use doesn't have to be dirt-cheap. The same design approaches can be applied to pricier components with great results. See the example of the IKEA-meets-Eames rocker on page 13.

Getting Organized

If you find yourself doing a lot of DIY projects, it's nice to have a selection of hardware on hand so you don't need to run to the store every time you need that odd screw. You can add to your stockpile by disassembling things that you're throwing away or recycling. Knobs, screws, handles, washers, gaskets, and so on are all worth scavenging if they are clean and in good shape.

If you know what you need but don't have it, you have to go looking. The first place to look is around your own home. Need a little dowel? How about a bamboo kabob stick from the kitchen? Need a bunch of small clamps? Go to the laundry room for a handful of clothes pins, or raid your desk for binder clips and rubber bands. Take an objective look at what you already have on hand and try to put it to use. Pretend you're MacGyver.

Sorting and Storage

Keep in mind that to be able to use this stuff, you need to be able to find it. It's no fun to have to dump out an entire coffee can of odds and ends to search for one little screw. Keeping things organized is a very good idea.

Look around your home for any equipment you need before rushing out to the hardware store. For example, you could use clothes pins or rubber bands as small clamps.

One way to do this is to buy a set of parts drawers. These are usually small racks filled with an array of little removable plastic drawers. This lets you sort things by type and size; say, little wood screws in this one, washers in that one, big screws in another one, and so on. You can then quickly hone in on the item you want, saving you the tedium of pawing through a big pile of things you don't need.

A homegrown alternative is to screw the lids of small jars (baby food or jelly jars work well) to the underside of a shelf. Simply fill the jars with hardware, buttons, bobbins, or whatever, and twist them into the lids so they hang in place below the shelf. While not as space-efficient as the drawers, this system is free and has been time-tested for decades in garages and basements.

Protect Yourself While Working

Odds are good that your raw materials will need some degree of preparation before they can be used in your project. This may include cutting them to size, repair, or at least a bit of cleaning. What is required will vary widely and depend on the material, its condition, and its ultimate use. However, all of these processes involve a degree of risk. Cutting, sanding, and grinding generate particles and dust. Cleaning and paint-stripping can involve harsh chemicals.

First off, you need to know how to use your tools safely and correctly. Where nifty tool techniques are needed in the projects in this book, we've included instructions, so follow these closely. Second, just as you accumulate a collection of tools to use to make your projects, you should also invest in appropriate protective gear. Use proper eye, respiratory, and hearing protection, and wear gloves, especially when using cleaners and solvents. Always follow the instructions on the product. Dust masks or respirators should be used when sanding or filing. There are different types for different uses. For example, the mask you use to protect yourself from dust won't protect you from paint fumes.

Household paints made before 1980 generally contain an amount of lead that is released as dust when sanded or scraped and inhaled into your body. You really want to avoid this. If you need to remove paint from items that date before this point, it is best done using a chemical stripper, of which there are several types on the market. In general, anything with cracked or peeling lead paint should not be allowed anywhere near children.

Dive In

Use the projects that follow to inspire you. No doubt you'll come up with your own bigger and better ideas as you look around your home and neighborhood for the cast-offs that can be transformed into stylish creations. Check out the Resources on page 142 for more help tracking down materials. Be safe. Be creative. Be resourceful. And have fun!

Time and Skill-Level Key

Each of the projects that follow is rated in terms of completion time needed and skill level.

Quick project, 1 hour max.

Medium-length project, allow a Sunday afternoon.

More ambitious project for which drying times and other waiting periods are necessary. This might take a weekend or so.

Skill level 1: Easy job for inexperienced re-creators.

Skill level 2: Requires some hardware and learning some handyman skills.

Skill level 3: Work up to these projects. You'll need to know how to keep your fingers away from the power saw (for example).

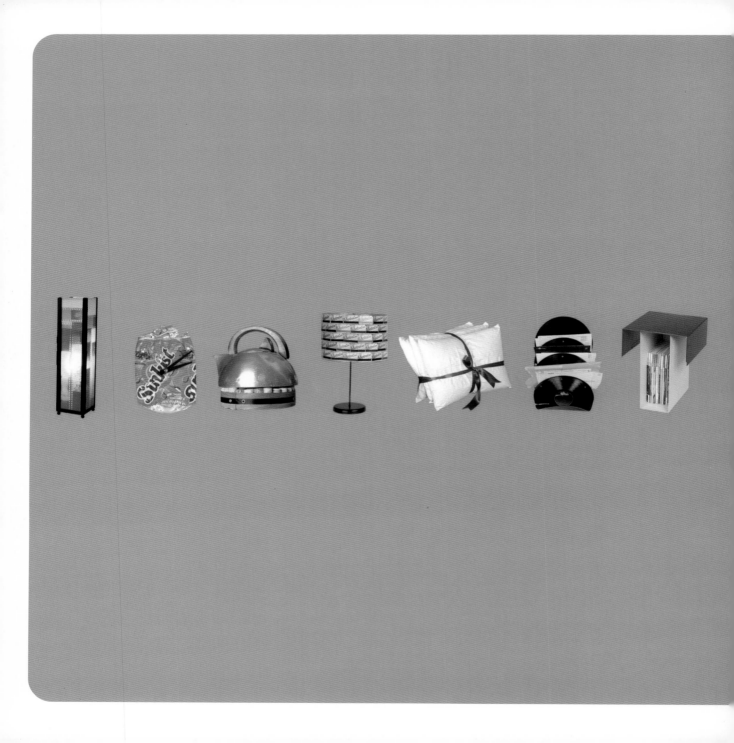

The Projects

License Plate Box

Materials

- 1 license plate
- 26-gauge galvanized steel sheet, 12" x 12"
- Scrap ½" thick plywood
- Wood finish (such as tung oil, paint, or clear polyurethane; optional)
- ¾" nails
- ½" pivot screws
- 4 washers to fit screws
- 4 stick-on rubber feet

see over for tools . . .

Make this simple "stuff" box, ideal as a pencil tin, by using an old license plate as its lid. The same processes can be applied to larger boxes, though an alternative material would have to be used for the lid. You could try using an old metal sign, for instance.

1. First, bend the very ends of the license plate down to form a "U" shape. Where the bend occurs will depend on the arrangement of letters on your particular plate, but the "legs" of the "U" need to be at least 1" long. Use the combination square to draw lines across the plate where the bends are located.

2. Clamp one end of the plate between two pieces of scrap wood, aligning the bend line with the edge of the wood. Then, pressing close to the bend line, fold the exposed portion of the plate over. Do the same for the other end of the plate.

3. Drill a ⅛" hole for the pivot screws in each of the legs at ½" from the bend line and ½" from the back edge of the leg.

4. Use tin snips to trim the steel sheet to a width of about ⅛" shorter than the distance between the bends in the license plate.

5. Mark a bend line 3¼" from each end of the steel. Following the same bending process as in step 2, make a 90-degree bend at each line to form the front, back, and base of the box.

6. Cut two pieces of plywood measuring 5½" x 3¼" to form the sides of the box.

7. The folds in the steel will be slightly rounded, so file the bottom corners of the wood pieces to match. Sand the pieces and apply

License Plate Box

Tools

- Combination square
- Pencil
- 2 bar clamps
- 2 pieces scrap hardwood or metal angle at least 8" long
- Electric drill with $\frac{1}{8}$" and $\frac{1}{16}$" bits
- Tin snips
- Handsaw
- File or sandpaper
- Hammer
- Punch
- Screwdriver

a finish to them, using tung oil, paint, or clear polyurethane, if you wish.

8. On the steel sheet front and back of the box, mark locations at each corner for the nails that will hold the sides in place. Dimple the locations with the hammer and punch, then pre-drill the nail hole with the $\frac{1}{16}$" bit.

9. Put the wood sides in place and drive the nails through the holes into the steel sheet and then into the wood.

10. Slip the cover into place on top of the box. The next step is to determine the location for the pivot screws. They need to be placed in a way that keeps the lid from binding when it is flipped up. Experiment a bit to find the right spot, then drill a $\frac{1}{16}$" hole into the ends of the box.

11. Screw the pivot screws into the wood sides with a washer between the wood and the license plate and another between the plate and the head of the screw.

12. Apply four rubber stick-on feet to the bottom of the box.

Necktie Cushion

Materials

- At least 12 men's ties
- 20" pillow form (or desired size)
- Lightweight iron-on interfacing
- Thread
- Embellishments, e.g. piping, cording, trim, buttons, fancy threads (optional)
- ¾ yd fabric for back of pillow
- 2¼ yd edging trim (optional)
- Pins
- Zipper (length determined by the size of cushion; optional)

see over for tools . . .

So you are getting rid of your scrappy old ties or, the man in your life is upgrading. To someone who sews, that means free fabric. But what can you do with a bunch of old ties? Here is a quick home furnishing project, which for intermediate or advanced sewers offers opportunities for quilting and embellishing. For those with intermediate sewing skills, the instructions on how to cut them up and make them into a throw pillow are easy to follow. Let your creativity take hold.

1. Wash the ties either by hand or in the washer. If you choose the washer, wash as many ties as possible at one time on the "delicates" cycle. To avoid pulling a huge knot of ties out at the end of the cycle, wash the ties within a pillowcase. Hang them separately to dry.

2. Cut the seam thread at both ends of each tie and pull it through. Discard the white stabilizer fabric. If you wish, cut off the points, and save them to use as an embellishment in this or a future project. Remove any lining material on the ties.

3. Iron the tie fabric on both sides. Because ties are cut on the bias, you will find that they stretch. To help prevent this from happening and to keep the edges from fraying, press some lightweight iron-on interfacing to the back of the fabric. You are now ready to cut the fabric into strips.

4. Decide how wide you wish to cut each strip to create your design. For the tie pillow shown on page 30, we used the rotary cutter to cut strips 2" wide along the full length of the ties. For information on how to use a rotary cutter, see Techniques (page 139).

Tools

- Scissors
- Iron
- Straightedge or quilter's ruler
- Rotary cutter
- Sewing machine

5. With right sides together, take a ¼" seam to sew the strips together and form blocks of fabric to your desired pattern. If the blocks don't quite fit the pillow form, consider adding a border to make up any difference. The blocks used in the pictured pillow are made up of three 2" strips stitched together and then trimmed to make 4½" squares.

6. The next step is to be creative. Quilt the top, use special stitching with fancy thread, cording, hand embroidery, machine embroidery, add buttons (regular or specialty)—whatever strikes your fancy.

7. Now complete the pillow cover. First cut the back fabric to the size of the pillow form, plus 1" extra on all sides. Pin the front to the back, right sides together.

8. To add piping around the edges, sandwich the piping between the decorated front cover and the back fabric facing inwards, and with fabrics right side together. Stitch a ¼" seam on three sides, using the zipper foot on the sewing machine. Leave the fourth side open.

9. If you plan to put in a zipper, use the zipper foot to stitch one side of the zipper along one open edge of the pillow cover. Turn the cover right-side out and then stitch the other side of the zipper to the remaining edge to complete. Insert the pillow form and zip up the open edge. If you do not wish to insert a zipper, simply slip-stitch the open side to complete.

Variation: Used Clothing Quilt

If you want to make a larger item, for example a quilt, you will need larger pieces of material such as all those old clothes that you no longer wear. Follow exactly the same steps as for the cushion but on a much larger scale.

Scrap Stone Candleholder

Materials

- Scrap limestone from a construction site
- Stick-on felt (optional)
- Candles

Tools

- Pencil
- Straightedge
- Electric drill with ¾" masonry bit
- Brush

A stout and unusual candleholder can be made from scrap building stone. Indiana limestone, as used in this example, is a common stone widely used for the exterior components of masonry building. It is relatively soft and easy to mill, making it possible to work with an electric drill using a masonry bit. Harder stones such as granite require more specialized equipment to shape them.

Look in Yellow Pages for building stone fabricators in your area. They generally have bins of scrap material and may be willing to give you a few pieces. If there is no usable stone available to you, you could achieve a similar look using a solid cinder block.

1. Based on the shape of the scrap stone, decide how many candles you want to use and where you want them to go. Use the pencil and straightedge to mark where you need to drill holes. Ensure that the stone will not tip over when the candles are installed.

2. Drill holes in the stone approximately 1" deep. In limestone or cinder block, it will be pretty easy work.

3. Blow the dust out of the holes, scrub the stone with a brush and water, and let it dry thoroughly.

4. Apply the adhesive felt to the bottom of the stone to avoid damaging any furniture it's set on.

5. Make sure the candles fit snugly in the base and aren't prone to tipping. If the hole is too small for the candle, you can use a knife to shave the base of the candle to the correct size. If the hole is too big, wrap the base with electrical tape until it fits the hole well. Of course, never leave candles burning unattended.

Floppy Disk Photo Holder

Time: 🕐	Skill: ↘

Materials

- Floppy disks
- Block of wood

Tools

- Glue

This is a simple and effective way to make use of all those obsolete floppy disks, which are ending up in landfills in very large numbers since we now use other methods of storage like CDs, or portable hard drives.

1. Remove the aluminum rectangle piece from the floppy carefully. For each photo holder you will need one of these aluminum rectangles.

2. For the base, you will need a block of wood. You could use a piece from a child's building block set, but old Lego or plastic blocks can also make good bases, or you can cut a piece of wood to fit. Make sure it is sufficiently weighty.

3. Glue the aluminum rectangle to one end of the wooden block, leaving the gap at the top to insert the photograph.

4. Once the glue is dry, your photograph holder is ready to use.

Tip You can also use these as place settings at dinner parties, placing a name card in the holder for each of your guests.

Tripod Lamp

Materials

- Aluminum tube ⅛" thick, 1½" square, 3" long
- Lamp socket with built-in switch
- Bulb
- Shade harp (support)
- 1" threaded lamp rod
- Nut or sleeve to fit lamp rod
- Plug
- Nut to fit tripod mounting screw
- Tripod
- Lamp shade

Tools

- Hacksaw
- File(s)
- Sandpaper
- Electric drill with bits
- Wire cutter/stripper
- Straight blade screwdriver

With just one piece of tube, you can turn a garage sale tripod into a surprisingly versatile lamp. By extending the legs, it can be converted from a table lamp to a floor lamp. Remove the shade and screw in a spotlight that can be pivoted by the tripod head.

And by removing one nut on the fixture you can use the tripod to hold a camera!

1. Cut the aluminum tube to size with the hacksaw and smooth the cut edges using a file and sandpaper.

2. 1" from the end of one face of the tube, drill a hole large enough for the mounting screw to pass through.

3. Drill a ½" hole in the opposite face of the tube and 1" from the other end.

4. File any burrs from the holes.

To wire the lamp socket:

5. Press the side of the socket where it says "press" and pull the socket apart, to make two halves. This will expose the internal base of the socket (see Fig. 1 and 2).

Fig. 1

6. Lamp cord consists of two parallel, insulated wires that are fused together. Slip the lamp base over the end of the cord; separate the two wires and then tie them together in a knot 2" from their ends. The knot

Fig. 2

should be big enough to prevent the cord from being pulled back through the base (see Fig. 3).

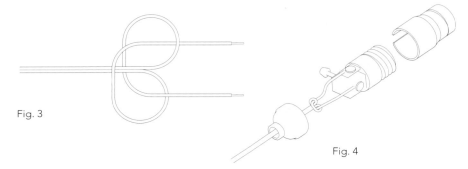

Fig. 3

Fig. 4

7. Cut the wires 1¼" beyond the knot and strip off from the end ½" of insulation. Twist the insulation as you slide it off to bind the internal strands of wire together.

8. Loosen the two screws on the sides of the socket. Bend one of the uninsulated wire ends into a hook shape and wrap it clockwise around the posts of one of the screws. It should wrap tight as you tighten up the screw. Do the same for the other wire and screw (see Fig. 4).

9. Slide the upper half of the socket down over the base and press the two together until you hear them click and lock in place. Make sure that no wires are pinched inside and that they aren't too crowded in the base. (See Fig. 5.)

Fig. 5

10. Thread the lamp rod into the base of the lamp socket and tighten the screw in the base to clamp the rod in place.

11. Run the end of the lamp cord through the shade harp (support) and then through the ½" hole in the tube. Slide the lamp rod through the hole in the base of the harp and then through the ½" hole in the tube. Slide the lamp rod nut over the cord, thread it onto the lamp rod, and draw it down tight.

12. Attach the plug to the end of the cord (follow the manufacturer's instructions).

13. Slip the smaller hole in the tube over the tripod mounting screw, and use the remaining nut to hold it in place.

14. Install the bulb and the shade and you're ready to go.

Plastic Strap Bench

Materials

- Poplar or other hardwood for:
  2 side rails: 1¼" x 1½" x 4½ ft
  2 end rails: 1¼" x 3½" x 12"
- ½" Phillips panhead screws
- Wood finish (such as tung oil or clear polyurethane; optional)
- Eight 2" #10 flathead wood screws
- 4 legs (scrounged, bought, or homemade), with screws
- ⅝" diameter dowel, 13" long
- Plastic strapping

see over for tools . . .

The heavy plastic strapping used for this bench seat was originally used to bind together large stacks of lumber during shipping. As you would imagine, it's pretty strong stuff. When the lumber arrives at its destination, the straps are cut and discarded. Take a quick walk through the aisles of a home center and you will find plenty of pieces either lying on the floor or about the racks. After a few visits, you can accumulate enough material to web a decent-sized bench.

The design shown in the picture opposite is a basic idea, but there are many ways to customize your own style. For example, shorten to make a stool, or use a different style of leg. The legs used here were scrounged from a pair of discarded chairs.

To build the frame:

1. Cut the dowel and the side and end rails to size.

2. At the midpoint of one of the 1½" faces of each side rail, drill a ½" deep hole. The diameter of the hole should match the diameter of the dowel. If your bench will be 2 feet or less in length, you can skip this step and eliminate the dowel.

3. Insert one end of the dowel in each of the holes and clamp the end rails between the side rails. Align the tops of the end pieces with the tops of the side pieces and let the side rails run 2" past the end rails (see Fig. 1).

4. Pre-drill, countersink, and install two screws, spaced 2" apart, through the side rails into each end of the end rails.

Fig. 1

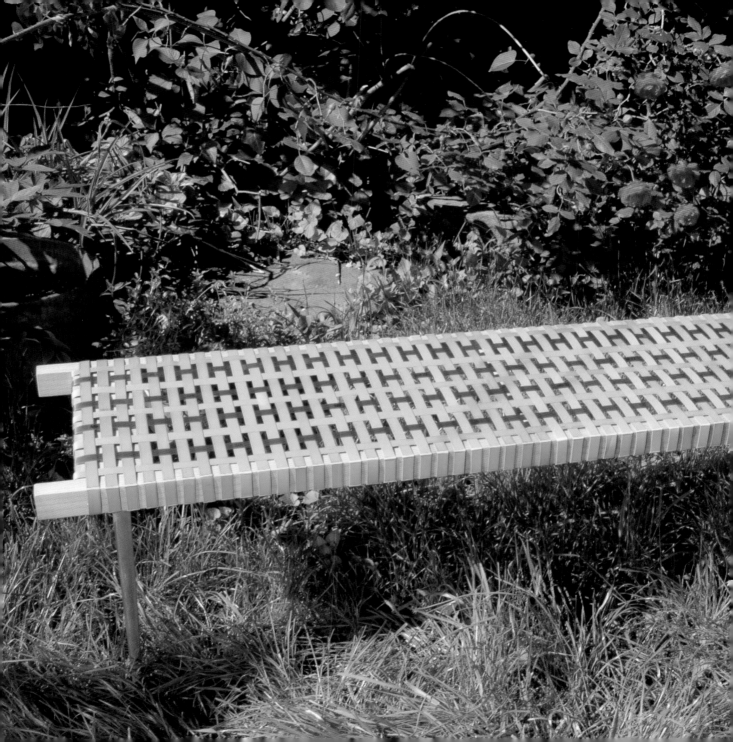

Tools

- Handsaw
- Electric drill with drill bits
- Screwdriver bit
- Two 18" bar clamps
- Fine file or sandpaper
- T-square or framing square (a sheet of poster board will work in a pinch)
- Tape measure
- Pencil
- Fine-tip marker pen
- Tin snips
- Pliers

5. Once the frame has been screwed together, sand the frame and apply a finish, if you like.

To prepare the straps:

6. Cut the straps into 21" lengths using the tin snips, and try to avoid any stains, labeling, or obvious damage. The number of straps required will depend on the length of the bench, but assume 12 straps for every foot of the bench's length, then cut a few extra. Also cut nine pieces that are each the length of the bench plus 9".

7. Place the frame on the floor or a table, with the underside facing up. Lay a strap across the middle of the bench and on the bottom of one of the side rails; mark with a pencil where the sides of the strap reach. From each mark, make additional marks at 1" intervals down the rail. Then lay the square across the frame and transfer these marks across onto the other rail. (At the ends you may need to tweak the interval a bit to get the straps to cover the heads of the screws that hold the frame together.) These marks will help you keep the straps straight and evenly spaced across the frame. Do the same thing on the end rails.

To install the straps:

8. Grip the end of a strap in the pliers 1½" from the end and fold the strap at 90 degrees, at a point right beside the pliers' jaws. Release the strap, and by hand, bend the fold further to 180 degrees, then squeeze the fold line with the pliers to crease the plastic.

9. Unfold the strap back to 90 degrees and align the short leg of the fold with the center strap marks on the underside of the frame. Use the drill with a screwdriver bit to drive one of the panhead screws through the strap into the frame (see Fig. 2).

10. Hold the strap up to the edge of the frame, mark where the next fold is to occur, pull the strap away, pinch it, fold it, and crimp it. Follow the same procedure until you've wrapped the strap around to the other side. Then screw the other end in place. Do this for all of the short straps. Before marking each fold, pull the strap tight to locate the mark correctly. The goal is to have the straps as taut as possible once both ends are screwed down. If a strap is too saggy, try to reinstall it or discard it and make a new one (see Fig. 3).

11. The process for attaching the long straps is similar: Just weave them between the short strips as you work from one end to the other.

12. Once all the straps are installed, use the tin snips to trim off any excess strapping on the underside of the frame. File any sharp corners on the cut ends of the straps.

13. Attach the legs to the underside of the end rails.

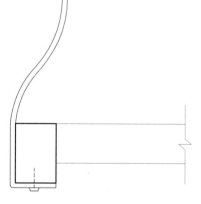

Fig. 2

Fig. 3

Pizza Pan Table

Materials

- 16" pizza pan
- Two 4 ft aluminum strips, ¾" x ⅛"
- 8 pop rivets
- One ½" machine screw and nut to fit

Tools

- Pencil
- Electric drill with ⅛" drill bit
- 2" wide masking tape
- 4" steel post
- Vise (or 1 bar clamp and 2 blocks of hardwood)
- Large piece of paper
- Combination square
- Compass
- Tape measure
- Scissors
- Pop riveter

Here's an ideal little table to hold your beer and chips while you're outside in the yard or inside, sitting on the living-room floor watching the game. It's all aluminum, so it's lightweight, weatherproof, and entirely recyclable. The aluminum strips are widely available in 4 ft lengths, so you can make the whole thing without having to do any cutting.

1. Draw reference lines across each of the aluminum strips as shown in Fig. 1. These will help ensure that the bends are made in the same spot on each of the table legs.

2. In the middle of the center mark on each strip, drill a ⅛" hole. Then drill holes ½" and 1¼" from each end of each strip.

3. On a piece of masking tape, draw three parallel lines, 1¼" apart. Then stick the tape onto the post. The post will be used as a form to bend the aluminum strips around. A 4" steel post (like you find in many home cellars) is ideal, but a rigid tube of some sort 3–4" in diameter will do the job.

4. Align mark A on one of the strips with the middle line on the tape. Bend the strip around the post until the B marks meet the outer marks on the tape. Do the same on the other end of the strip.

5. Align the center mark on the strip with the center mark on the tape and make the slight center bend.

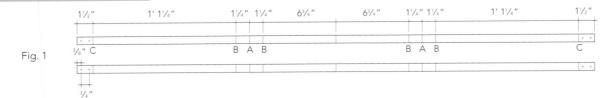

Fig. 1

1½"   1' 1¼"   1¼" 1¼"   6¾"   6¾"   1¼" 1¼"   1' 1¼"   1½"

⅜" C   B A B   B A B   C

¾"

Pizza Pan Table

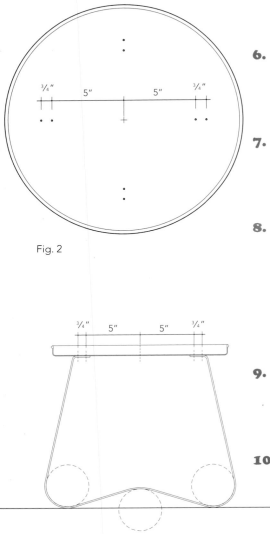

3/4" 5" 5" 3/4"

Fig. 2

3/4" 5" 5" 3/4"

Fig. 3

6. Clamp one end of the strip in the vise, aligning line C with the edge of the jaws, and make a sharp bend. Do the same on the other end of the strip. If no vise is available, clamp the bar between two blocks of hardwood instead.

7. Repeat steps 4–6 with the other strip. When the pieces are roughly formed, compare them to one another and fine-tune them until they match. Bend the curves tighter or open them up until they closely align with each other.

8. Drill holes in the pizza pan 5" and 5¾" from the center, at 12, 3, 6, and 9 o'clock. To lay out the hole locations, cut a piece of paper into a circle that fits just inside the rim of the pan. Fold the circle into quarters, cut two little notches in the edge, 5" and 5¾" from the center, then unfold the paper. Lay it in the pan and use the resulting openings in the paper to mark the hole locations on the pan (see Fig. 2).

9. Place one of the legs underneath the pan, align the holes in the pieces, and pop-rivet them together. Small screws can also be used, but the heads of the rivets are very flat, allowing you to set a glass right on top of them without rocking or tipping (see Fig. 3).

10. Once one leg is riveted to the pan, put the second in place and make sure the table doesn't rock. Adjust the middle bend of the second leg to keep the table from rocking, then rivet it to the pan as well.

11. Last, insert the screw through the holes where the legs overlap and tighten the nut.

Computer Case Table

Time: 🕐   **Skill:** ⌇⌇

Materials

- 2 CPU covers, one horizontal, one vertical
- 2 pieces wood, plywood, or MDF, each 8" x 18"
- Handful 6" x ¾" panhead screws
- Spray paint
- 4 rubber feet

Tools

- Tape measure
- Straightedge
- Pencil
- Handsaw or circular saw
- Electric drill with ⅛" drill bit
- Screwdriver
- File
- Medium to fine sandpaper
- Silicone sealant and caulk gun

In urban areas, it's common to see old computer cases (CPUs) set out with the trash. Fortunately, one of the simplest parts of a computer to reuse also happens to be one of the easiest to swipe off the curb: the big, dumb, U-shaped piece of metal that covers the chassis. They come in different sizes and depths and are shaped to cover either vertically or horizontally configured CPUs. Often these simply slide off from the rest of the computer or at most are held on with a few screws. Either way, you can easily grab yourself the makings of a new end table.

Alternately, if you don't want to scavenge, look in Yellow Pages for companies that recycle computers and components. They've usually got plenty of covers lying around. Net yourself a pair to make this simple little table/magazine rack.

1. Before you start, thoroughly wash the sheet metal pieces you've scrounged and leave them to dry while you cut the wood.

2. The table base is made from the vertical case and two pieces of wood that form its top and back. Cut both pieces of wood to match the case width. Cut the back piece to match the case height but cut the top piece 2" shy of the case's depth.

3. Slip the back piece into position as shown in Fig. 1. Attach the wood back by screwing into it through the existing holes in the metal at the rear of the case. Pre-drill screw holes in the wood first so that the wood doesn't split.

4. Drill two new holes in the upper edge of each side of the case and put the top piece of wood into place. Use the file to smooth off any burrs. The surface of the wood should sit flush with the

top edge of the case. Screw the wood through the new holes to attach the top.

5. To prepare the tabletop, set the horizontal case into position and drill two holes in the lip at its rear and file the holes smooth. You'll need these holes to attach the top to the base. Do not screw it in place yet.

6. Now paint the two halves of the table. A light sanding to take the sheen off the existing paint will help the new finish to adhere.

7. Once you've applied a few coats of paint, you can join the halves. First, use sandpaper to rough up the underside of the tabletop where it will rest on the base. Then, on the top of the base, squeeze out a few generous beads of silicone sealant, following the manufacturer's instructions. Center the tabletop on the base and install the last two screws. (See Fig. 2 and 3.)

8. Let the silicone cure, stick the rubber feet onto the bottom of the base, and then load the table up with your favorite magazines.

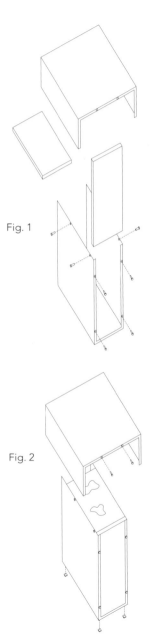

Fig. 1

Fig. 2

Fig. 3

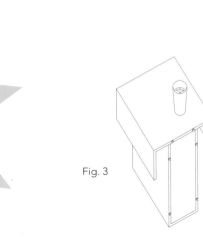

Foam Frame

Materials

- Foam packaging
- Glass or plastic to fit opening in foam
- Photograph
- Pins
- Bamboo skewer

Tools

- Bread knife
- Fine-tip marker pen
- Straightedge
- Scissors
- Craft glue or wood glue
- Glass cutter (if cutting your own glass)

Computers and electronic equipment come packaged in foam nests that protect them during shipping. The piece used here was packaging for a new hard drive and made for a simple frame almost right out of the box.

1. Find two pieces of foam, one with a recess that will form the frame and a second, flat piece for the prop on the back. With luck, the piece for the frame is ready to go as is. However, if you need to trim or shape a larger block of foam to get a usable piece, use a bread knife to cut it quickly and cleanly.

2. One edge of the prop will need to sit flat on the tabletop and an adjacent edge is to be glued perpendicular to the back of the frame. The prop needs to be roughly triangular shape. The frame needs to lean back to resist tipping over, so cut the edge of the prop at an angle. Experiment to find an angle that is suitable. It's a good idea to cut it oversize at first with a fairly steep angle. Draw a cutting line on the foam using the marker and straightedge and cut along it with the scissors. Attach the prop with the pins to try it out. If it's too steep, trim the edge back a little more.

3. Once everything is stable, trim any extra material off the prop piece. Remove the prop, apply the glue and put it back in place. Pin to hold it in place while the glue dries.

4. Cut the glass or plastic to fit into the opening in the frame. It ought to be just a little bigger than the opening, so the foam squeezes it when it is put in place over the photograph.

5. If necessary, insert a bamboo skewer into the prop to stiffen it.

Metrocard Lampshade

Time: 🕐	Skill: ⋏⋏

Materials

- Lots of cards
- Lots of jump rings ½"
  in diameter
- Scrap of plywood,
  approximately 8" x 12"
- Scrap cardboard
- Lampshade frame

Tools

- ¹⁄₁₆" hole punch
- Needle-nosed pliers
- Coping saw
- Strong rubber band
- Utility knife
- Tape
- Craft glue

Metrocards have taken the place of tokens in the New York City subway system and while they're reusable, it's inevitable that people accumulate expired ones. But you don't have to live in New York to make a similar lamp as the same process can be applied using old business cards, incomplete decks of playing cards, or baseball cards.

Take care to use a lampshade frame that will keep the cards well away from the light bulb. A large-size frame will also allow the cards to form a gentler curve and keep the lampshade from looking too faceted. Lampshade frames are available from craft stores, though you can reuse an old or damaged shade. The top and bottom hoops need to be the same size.

Aside from the cards and the frame, the other component of the shade is the jump rings. These are little wire rings used in jewelry making, which can be bought from craft stores.

The key to this project is to position the holes in the same place on all of the cards. The easiest and quickest way to do this accurately is to make a jig to punch the holes.

1. First, determine where the holes need to be on the cards. To hang them in the pattern shown here, you need to make holes at quarter and three-quarter points across the top and bottom of the cards. When the cards are clipped together, there should be a little space left between them. When you have a card that works well, mark it and put it aside to use as the master card.

To make the jig:

2. Use the coping saw to cut a "U" shape into the edge of the plywood so that the bottom jaw of the hole punch fits snugly into

it. You need the wood to prevent the punch from twisting or wobbling while still letting you squeeze the handles to punch holes.

3. Take the master card and close the hole punch on it so that the male half of the punch passes through the pre-punched hole. Wrap a rubber band around the handles of the punch to keep the jaws closed.

4. Take two pieces of cardboard and tack and glue them onto the wood alongside two edges of the card. Remove the rubber band and the punched card. This completes the jig.

To assemble the lampshade:

5. Place a new card against the edges of the cardboard on the jig, and punch a hole. Flip the card over and do the next corner and repeat until you have a hole in each corner of the card. Just make sure you don't let the card slip under the edges of the cardboard guides. Pop your favorite music on and punch all of your cards.

6. Once all the cards are punched, use the jump rings to clip them together. Open the rings by twisting them sideways. Don't pull them apart. When you close the rings, twist them back until you hear the ends click against each other. A pair of needle-nosed pliers will make the process easier on your fingers.

7. Attach the top ring of the shade frame to a lamp and start clipping the cards on, staggering the cards like bricks at each row. After a few rows, the pattern will begin to emerge. At the bottom of the shade, clip the cards to the bottom rim of the frame.

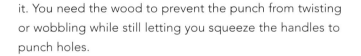

Novelty Clocks

Time: 🕐   **Skill:** ↖

Materials

- Item to use as the clock face
- Battery-operated clock movement

Tools

- Scrap wood
- Electric drill with selection of twist bits
- Needle-nose and regular pliers
- Wire cutters

A clock face can be made out of just about anything that you can drill a hole through—from roof slates to circuit boards, from LPs to books. All of the clocks shown here are based around a pre-assembled, self-contained movement (the mechanism that makes the clock run). These come in many degrees of complexity, accuracy, and cost, and are available with different length sleeves to accomodate clock faces of different thicknesses. If all you need is something to tell you how much time you have until Star Trek comes on, a simple AA battery-operated quartz movement will be fine. These can be purchased online and at most stores that sell craft or woodworking supplies.

Typically, the movement consists of a small plastic box which measures 2″ x 2″ and contains the moving parts and the battery. Connected to the center of the box is a threaded metal sleeve that is used to attach the movement to the face of the clock.

1. Once you've chosen your object for the clock, you need to drill a hole through its "face." The hole should be large enough to accommodate the threaded sleeve of the movement. However, if you're working with a tough material such as metal or dense plastic, start with a small drill bit and work up to the final size bit in a few steps. It will be easier to drill and will result in a cleaner hole.

2. The movement will come with the hardware required and installation instructions. Attaching the movement usually involves slipping a rubber washer over the threaded sleeve, poking the sleeve through the hole in the clock face, and threading a washer and a thin nut onto it. Then the hands are slipped on and a tiny retaining nut is screwed on. That's really all there is to it.

Novelty Clocks

Tea Tin Clock

This table clock started life as a tea tin picked up in a Chinese grocery. The fabrication is pretty straightforward and, in this case, the mouth of the tin was large enough to accommodate the movement. Make sure the hands are short enough to clear the table at 6.30.

Hubcap Clock

The hubcap clock is the simplest clock to attempt. It's really just a VW hubcap with a hole drilled in it. The movement has a slot molded into the back that allows it to hang on a wall.

LP or '45 Sleeve Clock

All you need to make this one is an old album sleeve, a utility knife, and some thick scrap cardboard. Two tabs were cut and folded out of the back to allow it to stand up. Some scrap cardboard was slipped into the jacket and glued into place for added rigidity.

Crushed Can Clock

The trick here is to squash the can in an aesthetically pleasing manner. So when you drive over it, place the side of the can against the tire tread and roll over it a few times. (If your neighbors don't already look at you strangely, this should do it.) Squash any remaining high spots with a pair of pliers.

TAYLOR

140 160
120 180
100 200
80 220
60 240
40 300 260
20 0 280

Scale Clock
A perpetually incorrect bathroom scale was gutted to make this clock. The internal springs were removed and the original dial was used as the face. Wire cutters were used to trim the hands to just the right length. Some tape and shims were used to hold the face in position before the scale was reassembled and hung on the bathroom wall.

Bucket Baskets

Time: ⊕ **Skill:** ⊼⊼⊼

Materials

- Large sheet of paper
- Two 5-gallon plastic buckets
- Cord or heavy string
- 10 rivets

Tools

- Pencil
- Ruler or straightedge
- Scissors
- Scotch tape
- Fine-tip marker pen
- Electric drill with $1/8$" and $3/8$" drill bits
- Electric jigsaw
- Utility knife
- Fine file
- 150- and 220-grit sandpaper
- Rivet tool
- Hammer
- Spring clamps or binder clips

Five-gallon plastic buckets are ubiquitous. They're used to hold paint, drywall compound, and even bulk food products. For this project, you'll need two buckets to make the large basket and the leftovers can be used to make up the smaller basket.

To make the large basket:

1. Reproduce patterns A and B from page 61 and cut them out. For the cross-shaped piece, cut it out like a paper snowflake: fold the sheet in half, and in half again, and then trace one quarter of the pattern onto the folded sheet (see Fig. 1). Cut out the pattern and unfold to reveal the whole template.

2. Remove the metal handles from the buckets.

3. Wrap the cross pattern (Pattern B) around one of the buckets and tape it in place, taking care to keep the centerline perpendicular to the bottom of the bucket (see Fig. 2).

4. Mark around the pattern onto the bucket using the marker, then remove the paper pattern. (When the long ends of the pattern wrap around, they meet at an angle due to the fact that the bucket tapers. Just round off this angle a little when tracing the pattern.)

5. Use the drill with the $3/8$" bit to make starter holes along the pattern line. Insert the blade of the jigsaw into a hole and carefully saw along the marker line to cut the shape out of the bucket.

6. Trace two of the trapezoid shapes (Pattern A) onto opposite sides of the second bucket. Align the wide end of the pattern with the bottom edge of the bucket rim, and mark as before. Drill a couple of starter holes, then cut out these shapes (see Fig. 3).

Bucket Baskets

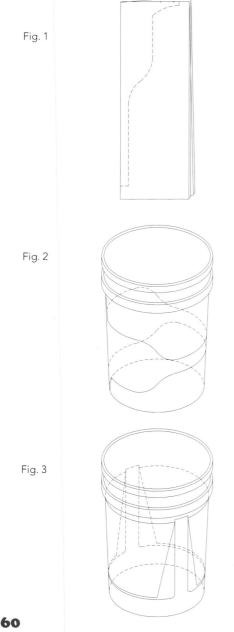

Fig. 1

Fig. 2

Fig. 3

7. Use the utility knife to fine-tune the cutouts if necessary, and sand all the edges with a fine file.

8. Drill two ⅛" holes in the tabs of the hoop piece (see pattern A). Center the wide edge of one of the trapezoid pieces on the base of the tab and drill two matching holes. Then, using the hammer and rivet tool, install two rivets to hold the pieces together. The tab should be on the outside face of the basket. Do the same with the other trapezoid piece.

9. Bend the tab to bring the ears of the trapezoid pieces up to the base of the handle. Make sure they line up evenly, then drill and rivet the ears to the handle base. It's helpful to clamp the pieces together during the drilling process.

10. Drill two ⅛" holes in the handle to provide a place to tie off the cord handle wrap, then wrap the handle with cord or string.

To make the small basket:

1. Use the leftover portion of the second bucket from which you cut the trapezoid pieces. Mark a line around the bucket 2" up from the bucket's base (see Fig. 3).

2. Lay out two 1½" wide handle strips vertically up opposite sides of the bucket. Round off the corner where the handle meets the base.

3. Cut the shape out of the bucket, sand the edges and round over the ends of the handle straps.

4. Bend the straps until they overlap and clamp them together. Drill a pair of holes and install two rivets to bind the handle straps.

Pattern A

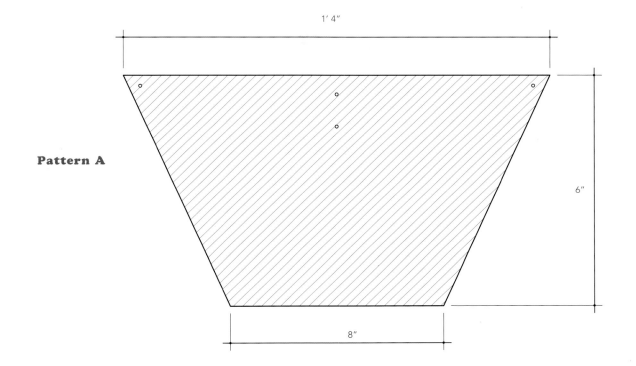

1' 4"

6"

8"

Pattern B

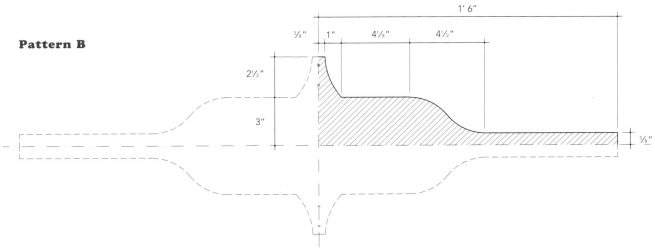

3/8"

1"   4 1/8"   4 1/2"

1' 6"

2 1/2"

3"

3/8"

CD Rack Table

Materials

- 2 wooden CD racks
- 2 sides of a wooden CD rack
- 8 screws
- Primer
- Black acrylic paint
- Printers type tray
- Two wooden blocks slightly smaller than the width of the tray and ¾" to 1" thick
- Wood glue

Tools

- Hacksaw
- Electric drill
- Screwdriver
- Paintbrush

As more and more of our music collections are stored on computers or MP3 players, we all have old CD racks going to waste. Instead of throwing them away, they can be used to create a beautiful new side table that also doubles as storage for all those CDs you can't quite bear to throw away.

To make the table base:

1. Use the hacksaw to cut the two sides of the CD rack to the width you require for the table. If the rack you're using doesn't have extra pieces left over to make the "bridges," you have a couple of other options you can use to create your table bases. Either cut pieces the correct size from scrap wood, or sandwich the towers between strips of lumber or sheets of plywood attached to the sides of the towers.

2. These pieces are used to form a bridge between the two CD towers to make the table more sturdy. One should sit about 3" underneath the table top, with the other about 3" from the bottom.

3. Make a mark on the CD towers where you want to attach the bridges and drill four holes for each bridge, then attach the bridges using the screws.

4. Paint the table base with primer, then follow with two coats of black acrylic paint.

CD Rack Table

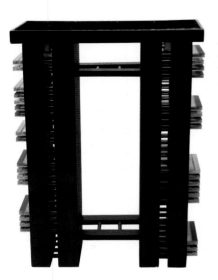

To make the table top:

5. The two wooden blocks are used to attach the table top to the CD rack base. Center the tray you are using for the table top over the table base and make a pencil mark to indicate where the blocks need to be glued to line up with the slots on the top of the two CD racks. This means the tray is removable, but will ensure that it fits over the base and does not slide or move around.

6. Glue the blocks to the bottom of the tray.

7. Prime the tray and then follow with two coats of black paint.

To decorate the table top:

8. This table is finished with a mosaic created from pages from a comic. To do something similar, follow the instructions for the decoupage tray on page 123. If a simple paint job is good enough for you, go get a snack and put your new table to use.

Tip Instead of comics or cartoons, photographs, wood, or carpet samples can be used to create a mosaic effect. An Asian look can be achieved by using a combination of red, gold, and black acrylic paints. Using origami paper and gold leaf would result in an expensive lacquer effect.

Stackable Cardboard Table

Time: 🕐   **Skill:** ↖

Materials

- Double wall corrugated cardboard
- Clear paste wax

Tools

- Utility knife
- Straightedge
- Pencil
- Wood glue
- Clothes pins or small clamps

Like the felt-covered table on page 86, these tables are made from double wall corrugated cardboard for maximum strength. Since they're entirely made out of cardboard, they are simple and cost practically nothing to make. Their shape also allows for them to be stacked on top of one another and nest together for storage.

For a more finished appearance than described, decoupage the surface with scraps of colored paper or magazine clippings (see page 123). Paint is another option, but experiment on scrap beforehand. Spray paint on cardboard rarely comes out looking good.

Alternatively, you could let your child go at it with finger paints. Play around. The table is basically free, so if you don't like the results, recycle it and make another one.

1. Reproduce patterns A and B from page 66. Using the knife and straightedge, cut the shapes from the corrugated cardboard as follows: Each table will require one piece of A and four pieces of B.

2. Score the pieces as shown by the dashed lines in the diagram. For tips on scoring cardboard cleanly, see Techniques (page 139).

3. Carefully fold the pieces along the score lines. The arms of the cross-shaped piece should swing down so their edges meet, forming the top and sides of the table.

4. Glue the legs inside the corners where the sides meet. In addition to supporting the table, the legs also serve to secure the joint between the sides. Clamp the pieces in place until the glue dries.

5. To protect the table against spills, rub on a coat of clear paste wax.

Stackable Cardboard Table

Pattern A

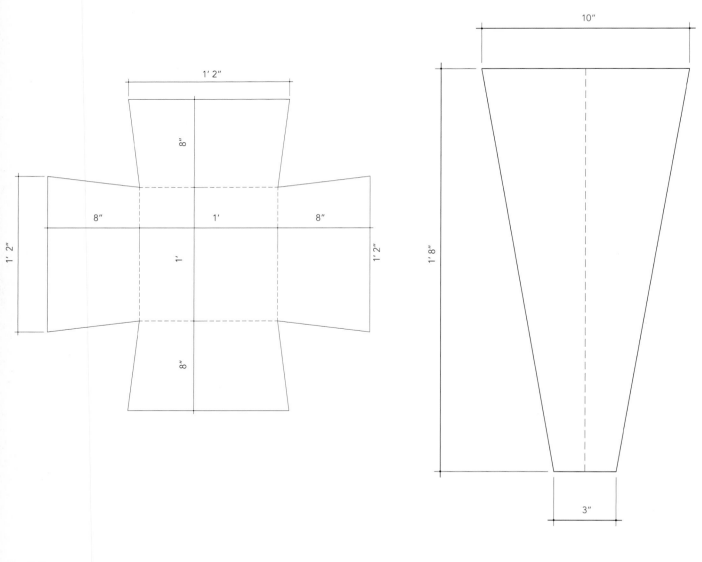

Pattern A measurements: 1' 2", 8", 8", 1', 8", 1' 2", 1' 2", 1', 8"

Pattern B

Pattern B measurements: 10", 1' 8", 3"

Negative Lamps

Materials

Time: 🕐   Skill: ↖

- Broken candle holder
- Sheet of perforated metal
- Lamp holder and mechanism
- Nuts and bolts
- Negatives
- Plastic folders

Tools

- Double-sided sellotape
- Scissors

Old or broken candle holders can have a new lease of life as lamps, recycling the electrical mechanism from any lamps that you no longer use. You can use any old negatives to create a sepia effect that looks really stunning when lit from within. However, be sure to use a small, low-wattage bulb and socket to avoid overheating.

Negative Tower

1. This lamp began life as a candleholder with one pane of glass missing. To replace a missing pane of glass, cut a piece of perforated metal to the same dimensions as the other panes and fit it to the lamp. The perforations will allow the light to come through and adds an industrial look that complements the negatives.

2. Attach the lamp mechanism to the the metal sheet using nuts and bolts.

3. Cut negatives to fit each side of the lamp. Make a random pattern for each side by using the negatives both horizontally and vertically.

4. Cut the plastic folders to the same dimensions as the panes of glass. Use double-sided sellotape to attach the negatives to the plastic, then sandwich the negatives between the plastic and the glass pane.

Hanging Negative Lamp

1. To make the second lamp, follow exactly the same procedure as for the negative tower, only this time using a hanging lantern.

2. To insert the negatives, remove the screws in the top of the lantern to remove the glass pane. Sandwich the negatives between the glass pane and the plastic folder before returning the panes to the lamp and screwing everything back into place.

Tip Colored tissue, transparent paper, skeleton leaves, or handmade paper can all be used to create interesting effects. To create an abstract pattern, use colored sellotape on paper. Parchment or greaseproof paper are good substitutes for the file covers. As always with lights, be careful not to let any flammable materials too close to a hot bulb.

Lawn Chair Wind Chime

Time: 🕐   **Skill:** ↖↖

Materials

- Lawn chair
- End cap for 4", schedule-40 PVC pipe
- Spool fishing line
- Wood ball 1½" in diameter
- An item to serve as a wind catcher
- 2 fishing swivels
- 1 metal or plastic ring
- 1 plastic bead

Tools

- Coarse file
- Pliers
- Tubing cutter
- 220-grit sandpaper
- Steel wool
- Electric drill with ⅛" drill bit
- Scissors
- Fine file
- Diagonal cutters

Eventually, the plastic webbing on lawn chairs gives out and splits. Rather than re-webbing them, owners tend to throw them out and buy new ones. While the plastic may be shot, the aluminum tubing is usually in fine shape and ripe for reuse. With some quick cutting and drilling, a backyard accessory can be converted into a new and alternative one.

1. Disassemble the chair. Use the file and pliers to remove the rivets holding any brackets in place.

2. Using the tubing cutter, cut the tube portions of the chair into straight pieces. The goal is to cut 6 pieces of tubing from the chair ranging from approximately 10" to 18" long, with each tube 1½" longer than the previous one.

3. Look over the pieces of tubing you've cut from the chair frame and trim them into the required lengths while trying to avoid any holes or dents in the tubes.

4. Wear a dust mask for protection, and lightly sand and buff each piece using sandpaper or steel wool.

5. Drill a ⅛" hole through each tube, ½" from each end.

6. Drill a ⅛" hole through the center of the PVC pipe's end cap. Then drill pairs of holes around the edge of the cap at the positions for 12, 2, 4, 6, 8, and 10 o'clock. At each location, the pair of holes should be ¼" on center.

7. Using the fishing line and the hole you've drilled, suspend the tubes below the end cap.

71

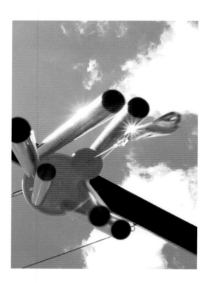

8. Tie additional loops of line around the holes in the cap at 2, 6, and 10 o'clock. Above the cap, tie each of the remaining ends together at a single fishing swivel.

9. Tie an 8" length of line to the ring and tie the other end of the line to the other end of the swivel.

10. To make the clapper, tie one end of a 12" line to the bead, and pass the free end down through the hole in the center of the end cap. Drill a hole in the wood ball and slip it over the end of the line, then tie the end to the second swivel. Tie a 6" length of line to the other end of the swivel. Then, on the other end of that line, tie on the wind catcher. In this case, a silver fishing lure was used, but anything with some weight and some surface area will work.

11. Lastly, use the tubing cutter to tune the "chimes." Cut off a little bit at a time until each has a pleasing tone.

Tip The six pieces of tube here were cut from one lawn chair. Cutting up an aluminum chaise longue instead will generate longer pieces for a more dramatic look and deeper tones. You could use any kind of hollow metal object for a different look and sound.

Wine Crate Table

Time: ◑   Skill: ⌇⌇⌇

Materials

- Hardwood (e.g. poplar) for:
  4 legs: 1" x 1" x 30"
  4 rails: 1" x 1", and the
  length needs to equal the
  widths of 3 crates + the
  width of 2 legs + 1"
  2 outer slats: 1" x 1" x 17¾"
  2 inner slats: ¾" x 3½" x
  17¾"
- Masonite for:
  2 side panels: ½" x 17¾" x
  height of the tallest crate
  + 1½"
  1 back panel: ½" x 17¾" x
  height of tallest crate + ½"
  1 base panel: ¼" x 17¾" x
  17¾"
- Scrap wood for guide strips:
  ⅜" x ⅜" x 17¾"
- Pine panel for tabletop
  2 x 4 ft
- #10 flathead wood screws
- Wooden knobs
- 4 rubber feet
  see over for tools . . .

This project was inspired by a tall credenza made up of old wine crates seen at a wine tasting.

You don't need to buy lots of vino to procure crates such as these. Just go to a well-stocked wine store and ask them nicely to save a few for you. Of course, you want the very prettiest (probably French) crates available. Here, the three wooden crates function as drawers. To expand the unit's storage potential, a shelf or one or two rows of drawers can easily be added below the top ones. It could form a very hip chest of drawers for a living room area or study.

All the wood remains unfinished and the screws are exposed to suit the raw quality of the crates. The concept is flexible and the wood thicknesses indicated are the minimum that will work, so play around with a design to match the crates you manage to get your hands on.

1. First, measure out and cut your wood and Masonite accurately, using the tape measure, combination square, and circular saw.

2. Construct the front and back frames as shown in Fig. 1, over the page. Pre-drill and install one #10 screw at each connection point. The distance between the top and bottom rail should be ½" more than the height of the tallest crate you have.

3. Pre-drill and screw the frames to the underside of the tabletop (see Fig. 2). The distance between the inside faces of each of the frames should equal the length of the slats.

4. Pre-drill and screw through the face frames to attach the slats. The inner slats should be centered on the gaps between the crates (see Fig. 3).

Wine Crate Table

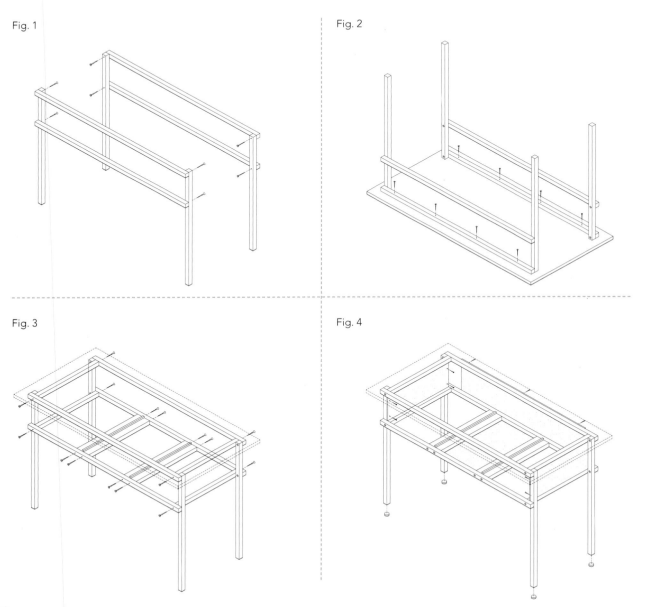

Fig. 1

Fig. 2

Fig. 3

Fig. 4

Tools

- Pencil
- Combination square
- Tape measure
- Circular saw
- Electric drill with drill bits
- Screwdriver or screwdriver bit for drill
- Wood glue
- Sandpaper

5. Glue the bottom panel to the underside of the inner slats (see Fig. 4).

6. At this point, the legs will want to rack sideways a bit. Adjust the legs so that they are square to the tabletop and screw the back panel in place. Then screw the side panels in place. These panels serve to stiffen the table.

7. Glue the guide strips in place on top of the inner slats so that they will fit between the crates and allow each crate to slide out easily, forming a drawer.

8. Drill a hole in the front of each crate and attach the wooden knobs to the crates (see Fig. 5).

9. Screw a rubber foot onto the bottom of each leg. Your table is ready!

Fig. 5

Plastic Bag Dispenser

Time: 🕐   **Skill:** ↖

Materials

- Towel
- Thread
- Pins
- Safety pins
- Cotton cord
- Elastic cord

Tools

- Sewing machine

This is a dual reuse project. Not only can you recycle a towel or an old pants leg to make it, but once you put it into use, it gives you a convenient place to store all of your plastic grocery bags until you can reuse them. While it won't add much to your home's décor, it will help you make your kitchen or pantry a bit less cluttered.

1. Fold the towel lengthwise and sew a ¼" seam along the long edge, to within 1" from each end.

2. At one end, fold back into the cylinder 1" of fabric, and sew ¼" from the edge to form a hem. Leave both ends of the hem open.

3. Clip a safety pin through one end of the cotton cord and work it through the hem to create a drawstring. Remove the safety pin and tie the ends of the cotton cord together.

4. Roll a cuff on the other end of the cylinder about 1½" wide. Sew ¼" from the edge to form a wide hem. Leave a gap at each end of 1".

5. Clip a safety pin through the end of the elastic cord and work it through this hem. Once it's through, pull on the elastic so that the end of the cylinder puckers. Overlap the ends of the elastic 1" or so and stitch them to secure.

6. Tuck the ends of the elastic back into the cuff and stitch up the last bit of the hem.

7. Turn the whole thing inside out and you're ready to fill it with bags. Stuff them in through the drawstring end and pull them out one by one through the hole in the bottom end.

Tied Rag Basket

Materials

- Steel rod ³⁄₁₆" in diameter, 3 ft long
- 3 pieces ¼" wire mesh:
  1 piece: 34" x 13"
  2 pieces: 10" x 11"
- 8 old T-shirts
- Plywood or Masonite, ¼" x 9½" x 14"
- 14" x 18" piece felt
- 2 wood strips, ¾" x 1" x 8"
- Four 1" wood screws

Tools

- Vise or locking pliers
- Electrical tape
- Tin snips
- Straightedge
- Rotary cutter
- Cutting mat
- Bucket or bag
- Long tweezers
- Craft glue
- Electric drill with screwdriver bit

When the edges of a good T-shirt or polo shirt get too frayed it is usually retired to the rag bin, but instead it can go towards making this tied rag basket. It takes a lot of fabric to make a rag rug, but a basket such as this offers the look on a more manageable scale.

It's sized to hold folders, paperwork, or magazines and is strong because the structure of the basket is a simple box made out of ¼" wire mesh, with a frame of bent metal to stiffen the top edges. A felt-covered Masonite panel is used to stiffen the bottom.

To make the basket frame:

1. Clamp the steel rod in a vise and bend it to form a 10" x 13" rectangle. Position the bends so the ends of the rod meet in the middle of one of the short sides. Wrap the point where the ends meet with electrical tape. This completes the frame that will stiffen the open face of the basket.

2. Cut the large piece of mesh to size using the tin snips.

3. Bend the mesh into a "U" shape to create sides of 7" x 13" and a base of 10" x 13". Then fold the top two rows of mesh squares around the steel frame.

4. Cut the two smaller pieces of wire mesh to fit the two ends of the "U" shape, using the tin snips. Bend each of the short edges and one of the long edges so that the piece slips into the end of the basket. (Use the mesh squares as a guide to determine the best fit.) Then fold the top two rows of the side pieces over the metal frame. You'll have to snip a couple of squares out of the upper corners to make it bend neatly.

Tied Rag Basket

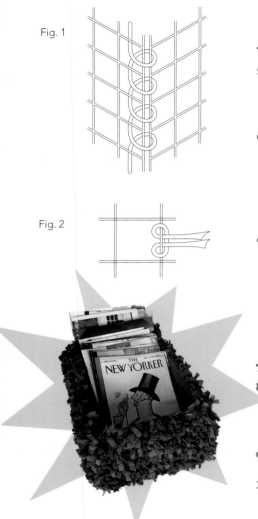

Fig. 1

Fig. 2

To rag the basket:

5. Use the rotary cutter and straightedge to cut ³⁄₈" wide strips from the T-shirts. Each strip needs to be 3³⁄₄" long. Mix up the colored strips really well in a basket afterward.

6. Cut four 12" long pieces of T-shirt material to tie the corners of the mesh together. Loop a strip around two adjacent squares, pull tight, and draw the end of the strip down through the next square as shown in Fig. 1. Continue wrapping all the way down the edge and tie it off at the end. Do the same at all four corners.

7. Start at the upper right-hand corner of one side and loop one of the 3³⁄₄" strips around the wire as shown in Fig. 2. Loop strips around all the vertical wires in the mesh and also around the top edge of the steel frame. A pair of long tweezers or a crochet hook can make this a bit easier.

To finish:

8. Cut the Masonite panel so that it fits into the base of the basket. Set the panel into the middle of the felt square. Fold the edges over on to the panel and glue in place.

9. Place the panel in the bottom of the basket, felt facing upward.

10. The wood strips are used as feet. Place one under each end of the basket. At each foot, drive two screws down through the bottom panel and into the top of the leg.

Variation: Tied Rag Rug

Use the same technique—and a lot more clothes—to create a rug. Instead of using the mesh to form a basket, simply cut a piece to the size you require and the attach the rags using the method above.

Window Sash Bookcase

Materials

- 2 window sashes
- Plywood or MDF—sizing dependent on size of sashes
- 4 feet or casters
- Wood screws
- Wood glue
- ½" nails
- 1" finish nails
- Two 8 ft pieces of ½" x ½" x ⅟₁₆" aluminum angle
- Four 8 ft pieces of pine quarter round molding

see over for tools . . .

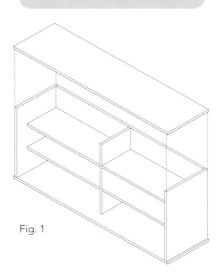

Fig. 1

Using window sashes as sliding doors can liven up a basic bookcase. The key is to build the top, bottom, and sides extra deep to accommodate the thickness of the sashes.

The bookcase illustrated is a quick and basic version built from MDF, which is essentially recycled sawdust. Available in 4" x 8" sheets, it's inexpensive, very flat, and takes paint well. The downside is that it's heavy. The sashes were used as they were found, getting just a wash before they were installed.

The tracks in which the sashes slide are quite simple. The edges are strips of ½" quarter round molding and the middle divider is a length of ½" x ½" aluminum angle. The lengths and how far apart they are mounted will depend on the sashes you use.

The same basic idea can be applied to a more finished piece by repainting the sashes and using higher quality materials.

1. Obtain two window sashes, clean them, and paint them if desired.

2. Set them end to end and measure the overall width and length. Add ¼" to the shorter dimension and subtract 2" from the longer dimension. This will be the size of the back of the bookcase.

3. The sides are 18" wide and their height matches the height of the back. Also, cut a middle divider the same height and 9" wide.

4. The top and bottom are 18" wide and 3" longer than the back.

5. Cut the pieces to size and screw the back, sides, top, and bottom together to form a box. The back fits between the sides, which in turn fit between the top and bottom pieces. (The top and bottom should overhang the front and sides of the cabinet.) Then screw

Tools

- Tape measure
- Straightedge
- Combination square
- Power drill
- $\frac{1}{8}$" bit
- $\frac{1}{16}$" bit
- Countersink bit
- Screwdriver bit
- Pencil
- Sandpaper
- Circular saw or tablesaw
- Handsaw
- Hacksaw

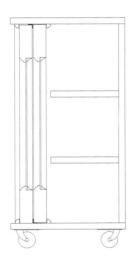

Fig. 2

the middle divider in place as shown in Fig. 1. For best results when working with MDF, predrill all of the holes and avoid driving a screw into the edge of the panels less than 2" from any corner.

6. Cut as many 9" wide shelves as desired and glue 9" long pieces of quarter round molding to the divider and sides to serve as shelf supports. Set the shelves in place.

7. Sand the edges of all the pieces.

8. Cut the quarter round and aluminum angle to match the length of the back panel of the bookcase. Drill a series of holes along one leg of the angle 18" apart using the $\frac{1}{16}$" bit.

9. Nail and glue the angle and quarter round to the top and bottom as shown in the cross section side view in Fig. 2. Install the innermost quarter round first. Then put a sash in place. Nail through the holes in the angles to fix them in place as shown in the diagram. Then set the second sash in place and install the outer quarter round. Leave enough space between the components to allow the sashes to slide. If they bind a little, lubricate the tracks with some paste wax.

10. Lastly, screw the feet or casters to the bottom of the cabinet. Depending on the length of your cabinet, an extra foot may be needed in the middle of the bottom to support the center of the cabinet.

Felt-Covered Table

Materials

- 1½ yd felt or other heavy fabric, such as cotton duck or twill
- Thread
- Pins
- Scrap double wall cardboard
- Packing tape
- Scrap wood for 4 legs, each 1" x 1" x 12"
- 4 rubber feet

Tools

- Tape measure
- Scissors
- Sewing machine
- Straightedge
- Pencil
- Utility knife
- Wood glue
- Screwdriver

Ever wonder why people buy expensive furniture only to hide it with slipcovers? Why not make a nice slipcover and put it over something cheap and simple?

That's the idea behind this table, which consists mostly of corrugated cardboard. The legs are lengths of scrap wood glued into a cardboard carcass, and to give the whole thing a tactile quality, the slipcover is made of felt. If the table wears out, you can recycle it and build a new one very easily.

The body of the table measures 14" x 14" square x 21" high, and for simplicity that's how we'll describe things here. Of course, you can adjust the measurements to build to a different design using the same materials. For best results, size the cardboard panels so that they fit inside your slipcover snugly. Keep in mind that it's easier to make the table fit the cover rather than make the cover to fit the table.

To make the slipcover:

1. Cut one piece of felt 57" long x 22" wide and a second piece 15" x 15" square.

2. Bring the two short ends of the long piece together to overlap each other by ¾". Pin and sew two lines of stitching along the overlap to fasten the ends together. You will have a large cylinder of felt. (See Fig. 1.)

3. Next add a bottom to the cylinder. Take the square piece of felt and position the middle of one of the edges against the end of the seam stitched in the cylinder, keeping right sides together. Pin the two together taking a ½" seam allowance. Then work your

Felt-Covered Table

Fig. 1

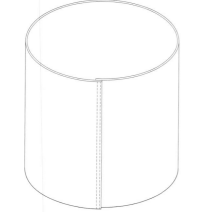

way along, pinning the two pieces together until the edge of the square is pinned to the edge of the cylinder.

4. Stitch along the line of pins, taking a ³⁄₈″ seam. Remove the pins.

5. Repeat steps 3 and 4 with each edge of the square of felt, until each side is sewn to the cylinder.

6. To finish, fold the edge at the open end of the cylinder over to the outside to make a ¹⁄₂″ cuff. Pin and stitch ¹⁄₄″ from the edge to make a hem around the top edge of the bag.

7. Turn the bag inside out and it's done.

To make the box:

8. Cut a 14″ x 14″ square of cardboard for the top.

9. Cut two 21″ x 14″ pieces of cardboard for the side panels. Two further side panels should be cut 21″ long and 14″ wide but less twice the thickness of the cardboard. For example, if the cardboard is ¹⁄₄″ thick, then the width of the panel should be cut 13¹⁄₂″ wide.

10. Cut eight 4″ x 8″ pieces of cardboard. The corrugations should run parallel to the short side. Score each strip lengthwise, down the middle, and fold the pieces into "L" shapes. For advice on scoring cardboard, see Techniques (page 139).

To assemble the table:

11. Carefully tape the long edges of the four side panels together to form a long tube. The wider sides should be placed opposite

Fig. 2

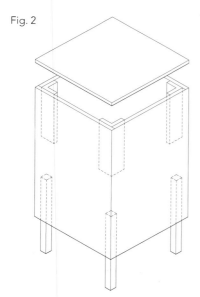

each other and should overlap the edges of the narrower panels. (See Fig. 2.)

12. Arrange the sides accurately and position the top to line up nicely on all four edges at one end. Tape the top panel in place, and where two pieces of cardboard meet at each edge, tape them completely. Before you go further, slide the slipcover over the box to make sure you're happy with the fit.

13. If all is well, flip the box over so you can reach the inside and glue the L-shaped pieces into the joint where the top meets the sides and where the sides meet each other. Avoid locating the L pieces where the legs will be attached.

14. Using a tape, measure and mark 14" up from the top panel in each corner. Now, glue the four wooden legs to the inside corners in the lower half of the box using the marks as the guide to ensure the table legs are level. Clamp the legs in place while the glue dries.

15. Once the glue dries and the legs are secure, screw the rubber feet onto the bottom of the legs. Flip the table over, slide the slipcover on, and smooth out any wrinkles.

Tip Cut a piece of ¼" thick plywood the size of the tabletop and lightly glue it to the top of the table before you put on the slip cover. This will provide some added durability and make it sound more substantial when you set a glass down on it.

Wine Cork Trivet

Time: 🕐   **Skill:** ⋌⋌

Materials

- Walnut wood strip 24" x 1½" x ¹⁄₁₆" (used in model making and available from hobby stores)
- Plastic tube or pipe 2" in diameter, 30" long
- Wood finish (such as tung oil or wax)
- Metal crate strapping ½" wide, 28" long
- Block of scrap wood
- Six ¼" grommets
- 75 wine corks

        see over for tools . . .

It may take a while, or at least a few good parties, to accumulate sufficient corks to make a decent size trivet, but once you have, you can put them to work protecting your tabletop from hot dishes.

Two concentric bands hold the trivet together. The outer band, made from metal crate strapping, provides strength. The inner wooden ring stabilizes the corks. The two are held together with small grommets and the corks are held in place by friction when they are squeezed into the rings.

Metal strapping is used to secure cartons during shipping and your local lumber yard or home center is a good place to find some.

1. Trim the walnut wood strip to size using a utility knife and straightedge.

2. Plug the bottom of the plastic tube or pipe and wrap it well with duct tape. The idea is to make it watertight.

3. Run the kitchen faucet until the water is hot. Drop the wood strip into the tube and carefully fill the tube with hot water. The wood will want to float to the top, so push a pair of serving tongs or a bent coathanger into the tube to hold it down.

4. Stand the tube in the sink in case the bottom starts to leak and leave the wood in the water for 10 minutes or so until the water cools. It's important to keep the wood submerged, so if water does leak out, keep it topped up.

5. Remove the wood from the water and carefully wrap it around a cooking pot (see Fig. 1). Use the spring clamps or belt to keep the wood wrapped tightly around the pot and leave overnight to dry.

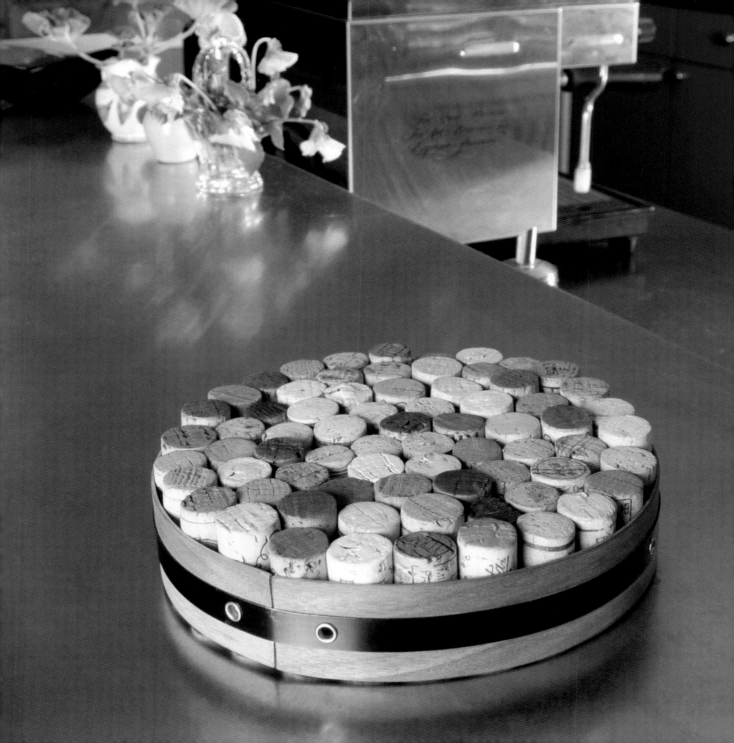

Wine Cork Trivet

Tools

- Utility knife
- Metal ruler or straightedge
- Duct tape
- Cooking pot 8"
  in diameter
- Spring clamps or a wide
  web belt
- 220-grit sandpaper
- Masking tape
- Pencil
- Centerpunch
- Hammer
- Electric drilll with ⅛" and
  ¼" drill bits
- Grommet tool
- Awl
- Tin snips

6. Remove the clamps and slide the wood from the pot. You should have a nice wooden ring. Don't worry if the ends don't quite touch. If the wood is basically circular, it will work. Sand the wood and coat it with a finish such as tung oil or wax.

7. Wrap masking tape around the end of the metal strap. Make a mark in the middle of the strap about ½" from the end and make another mark 1½" further down.

8. Place the strap on a block of scrap wood and set the tip of the centerpunch on one of the marks you just made. Strike the punch with the hammer to create a dimple in the strap. Drill a ⅛" hole centered on the dimple, and then enlarge the hole using the ¼" bit. Repeat the process at the other mark.

9. Wrap the metal strap around the wood ring and tighten it until the ends of the wood touch (see Fig. 2). Ensure the ends of the metal strap with holes overlap on the outside. Mark the centers of these holes on the underlying end and drill these as before.

10. Wrap the strap again until the holes line up and slip one of the grommets through temporarily. Place the wooden ring inside the strap. The ends should just touch or slightly overlap. If they do overlap, trim one of the ends slightly.

11. Remove the wood and hold the looped strap in front of you with the pair of holes at 12 o'clock.

12. Unloop the strap and drill an identical pair of holes at 6 o'clock and a single hole at both 3 and 9 o'clock.

13. Install a grommet at the end of the strap, align the holes, and crimp it into place. Your strap is now a ring.

14. Insert the wooden ring inside the metal ring. The joint between the ends of the wood should be centered between the pair of holes you drilled at 6 o'clock. Adjust the metal ring so it's in the middle of the wooden ring (widthwise) and mark the centers of all the remaining holes on the wood ring.

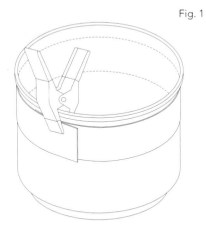

Fig. 1

15. Using the awl (or the tip of a nail or screw), make a dimple in the wood at all the marks you just make. (Don't use a hammer—just use hand pressure to avoid splitting the wood.) Drill the holes using the ¼" bit.

16. Wrap the wooden ring within the metal one and line up the holes. Crimp a grommet in each hole, locking the wooden and metal rings together.

17. Now start wedging the wine corks into the perimeter ring. At first the ring will be oval, but squish it a bit and try to rearrange the corks so they form concentric circles. Corks are slightly different sizes, so rearrange them until they all fit snugly. If a few are too long, trim them with a utility knife. The bits you slice off can be used as shims to wedge the corks tighter.

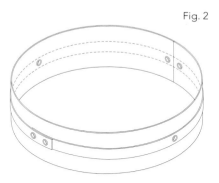

Fig. 2

18. When all the corks fit tightly and you can lift the trivet without any falling out, you're done. Brew up a pot of tea and try it out.

Tip The warmth of the hot water softens the fibers of the wood and makes them more pliable and willing to bend. Bigger pieces of wood used for furniture are cooked in steam boxes to achieve the same effect. In this case, the wood is thin so the hot water does the job. Sometimes the wood cracks in the process of bending, but don't be discouraged—it happens. Just try again with another piece.

Stone Drawer Pulls

Time: 🕐 **Skill:** ⚒

Materials

- Aluminum tube, ⅜" in diameter
- Attractive stones or pebbles, at least ⅝" thick
- Threaded rod, ⅛" in diameter
- Spacers
- Rubber washers, ¼" in diameter
- Metal washer to fit over rod
- Acorn nut to fit rod

Tools

- Tubing cutter
- Electric drill with ¼" masonry bit
- Hacksaw
- Fine file or fine steel wool
- Epoxy glue
- Small piece scrap wood
- Stick
- Baby oil
- Clamp

A beautiful accent to a plain piece of furniture can be the addition of some interesting hardware, and drawer pulls are a quick way to achieve this. Making your own gives the piece even more appeal, especially if it offers a way of bringing nature indoors.

Next time you're at the beach or on a hike, pick up a few interesting stones to use. Collect more than you think you'll need as some may be too hard to drill. Look for visible sedimentation lines in the stones as there's a good chance you can drill into this more easily.

1. Buff the aluminum tube and use the tubing cutter to trim off a piece ½" long.

2. Drill a ¼" hole approximately ⅜" deep into the back of the stone.

3. With a hacksaw, cut off a piece of threaded rod. Note: the required length of the rod depends on the thickness of the drawer or door you are fitting. To determine the length, insert the rod into the stone and slide the spacer and washers over it as described in step 7. Then add the thickness dimension of the drawer plus an extra ⅛". Cut to size, and file any burrs from the ends.

4. Scrub the stone clean with a brush and water and let it dry thoroughly.

5. Mix some epoxy glue on a piece of scrap wood and use a stick to spoon it into the hole in the stone, filling it to about halfway.

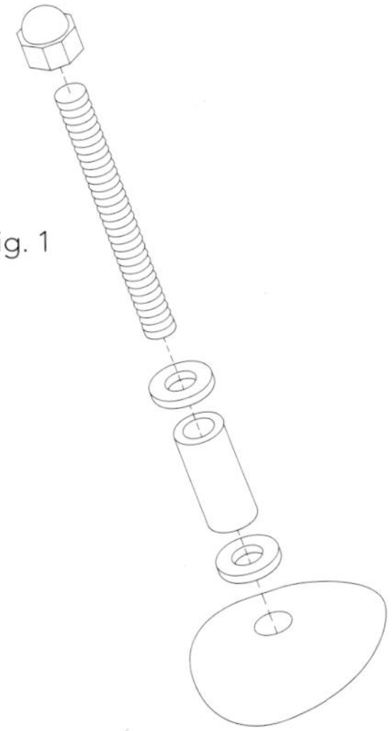

Fig. 1

6. Slowly insert the threaded rod into the hole, twisting and wiggling it to work out any air bubbles. Clean away any epoxy that gets on the stone as it will darken that area. Hold the rod in place until the epoxy cures. As it starts to stiffen, fine-tune the position of the rod, making it perpendicular to the back of the stone.

7. When the epoxy has cured, rub some baby oil into the surface of the stone to darken it and make its colors more visible. This will also help reduce staining from fingerprints.

8. Slip a rubber washer over the knob's threaded rod, then the aluminum spacer, and then another rubber washer. Slide the rod through the hole in the door or drawer front, then slide on the metal washer and thread the acorn nut onto the end to fix the whole thing in place. (See Fig. 1.)

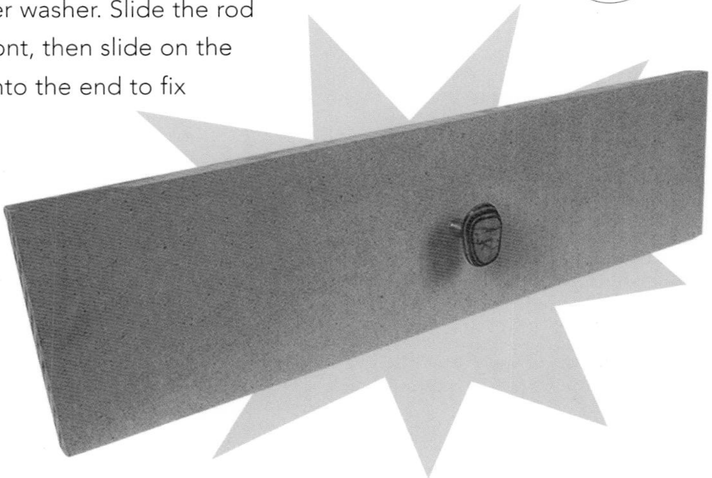

Tip The same basic idea can be used to make pulls from other found objects. Some potential resources are billiard balls, scraps of driftwood, champagne corks, or small toys or figures. Any reasonable small item that a ³/₈" deep hole can be drilled into has potential.

Junk Mail Pillows

Time: 🕐   **Skill:** ↖

Materials

- Large mailing envelopes
- Shredded paper
- Needle and thread

Tools

- Scissors
- Sewing machine
- Dowel or stick

For once, allow your junk mail to help bring you some relaxation instead of stress. Once you've shredded it, use it as filling for a throw pillow on which you can rest up before paying the real bills.

These steps will give you a rectangular pillow, but the same process can be used to make a free-form-shaped pillow. Just stitch a blob shape instead of a rectangle and then trim the excess envelope away, leaving about ½" of material beyond the stitch line.

1. Trim off the flap of the envelope.

2. Thread-stitch around the perimeter of the envelope, but stop short by 3" before the starting point to leave a gap in the stitching.

3. Snip the four corners off the envelope and then turn it inside out.

4. Stuff the envelope full of shredded paper, using a dowel or stick to get the stuffing into the corners. When it's fairly densely packed, sew up the 3" opening by hand.

Tip For best results, use spun polyester (Tyvek) envelopes for durability. A common source of these are the hard to tear (but seldom reusable) envelopes often used by courier companies.

Cardboard Tube Vases

Time: 🕐   Skill: ꜩꜩ

Materials

- Cardboard tubes
- Sheet of paper
- Plastic or metal strapping
- Small grommets
- Plastic soda bottles
- Flowers

Tools

- Pencil
- Utility knife
- Sandpaper
- Tin snips
- Fine file
- Punch (for metal strapping) or awl (for plastic strapping)
- Masking tape
- Electric drill with drill bits
- Grommet tool

These vases are versatile. The short vase can sit on a table or hang from a hook on the wall, while the longer vase can hang from the wall with the flowers displayed out of its side. To display fresh flowers, insert a plastic container into the tube to hold water.

Cardboard tubes are used for packaging or as the cores in rolled products such as carpet, fabric and paper. Good sources are carpet companies, fabric shops, or reprographic shops.

The metal and plastic strapping used here can often be pulled out of the lumber racks at your local home center. (Avoid strapping that was wrapped around pressure-treated lumber, though.)

To make the short vase:

1. To cut the tube to the desired length, first make a cutting guideline. Wrap a sheet of paper around the tube so that the edges align all the way around, then mark onto the tube along the edge of the paper. Carefully score along the marked line with a utility knife, and keep working your way around the tube until it is cut through. For advice on scoring cardboard, see Techniques (page 139).

2. Using the scoring method again, cut two notches in the bottom of the tube slightly wider than the strapping.

3. Lightly sand the cut edges to even them out and remove any fuzzy bits.

4. Clean the strapping and cut it into manageable lengths using tin snips. Be careful, metal strapping is springy and cut edges can be sharp. Use a file to dull the sharp ends.

5. Cut a piece of strap long enough to wrap around the outside of the tube and allow the ends to overlap 1½".

6. Use an awl or punch to start a hole ⅜" from one end of the strap. Drill the hole large enough to accommodate the grommet. Metal straps are tough, so start by first drilling a small hole, and then enlarging it to the required size. It's also helpful to wrap the end of the metal straps with masking tape to make any marks you use to locate the holes easier to see.

7. Wrap the strap around the tube and find where the hole in the other end needs to be. The loop should be loose enough to allow a piece of strap to slip between it and the tube. Drill the second hole and then trim off the extra length.

8. Line up the holes and insert a grommet. Use the grommet tool to crimp it in place and lock the two ends together.

9. Determine how long you want the "J"-shaped strap to be and cut an appropriate length of strap. Drill a hole ⅜" from each end.

10. Make two bends in the strap to form a "J" shape. The short leg of the "J" runs up the front of the tube; the longer one runs up the back between the tune and the loop.

11. Slip the "J" and the loop into place around the tube and mark the spot on the front of the loop where the two intersect. Drill a hole in the loop, then grommet the two pieces together. Install a grommet in the hole at the other end of the "J."

12. Slip the tube into place.

13. Cut off the top of a plastic soda bottle, just below the neck, and slip this into the tube, to hold the water for your flowers.

To make the tall vase:

1. The long tube vase (right) is simpler to make than the shorter version. Start with a long tube and cut the "window" with a utility knife (see Fig. 1).

2. Drill a hole near the top end of the tube to use to hang it onto a wall hook.

3. Drill two pairs of holes to accommodate the rods as shown in Fig. 1. The upper rod helps support the stems. The lower rod supports a cut-off plastic bottle used to hold water and the flowers (as above). Use an interesting material for the rods; for example, pencils, twigs, bamboo, or scrap metal.

3. Pull the bottom rod out to remove or insert the water bottle.

Fig. 1

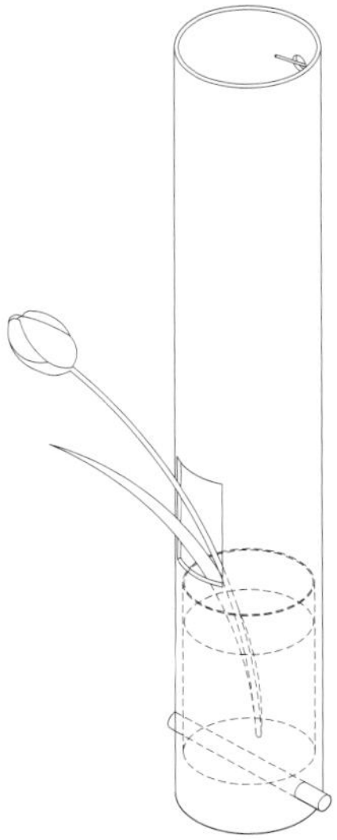

Mosaic Bowl

Time: 🕐   **Skill:** ↖

Materials

- Aluminum plate
- Magazines, brochures, or photographs

Tools

- Silver spray paint
- PVA glue
- Matte acrylic varnish
- Fine grade sandpaper

Old magazines and photographs can be used to create stunning mosaics that transform old objects. For this example, an old aluminum plate that was found in a dumpster was used, but you could use an old tray or something similar.

1. Clean the plate thoroughly, then paint the front of the plate using silver spray paint.

2. Cut up pictures from magazines, brochures, or old photographs into approximately ½″ squares, choosing your color scheme before you start. This plate uses blues and turquoises, cut up from photographs of the sky and the sea in tourist brochures.

3. Glue the squares to the surface of the plate to create a mosaic effect.

4. To make the dish waterproof, apply 5–6 coats of matte acrylic varnish, sanding lightly using a very fine sandpaper after every two coats.

Tip To create a very interesting textured effect, you could cut up old architectural plans or maps instead of photographs. Alternatively, you could use pictures of wood samples to simulate a wood inlay.

Found Object Fruit Bowls

Time: 🕐   **Skill:** ⚒

Materials

- Electric fan cover
- Rubber or cork coaster
- Stainless steel blender attachment
- Wok lid
- Stainless steel toilet roll holder

Tools

- Awl
- Nuts, bolts, and washers

Fruit bowls can be made using a variety of found objects. Inevitably, there will be several pieces of home and kitchen equipment lying around the house, or that you can easily scavenge, that no longer work. You can use old fans, blenders, woks, lids, or anything really, to create simple but stylish fruit bowls. These projects use an electric fan and a wok.

Electric Fan Bowl

1. The basic container of this fruit bowl was made using the cover of an electric fan that was no longer working. The base was made from a stainless steel blender attachment.

2. Cut a circle 3" in diameter from a piece of rubber—you could use a rubber or cork coaster—and place it in the uneven depression in the center of the fan cover.

3. Punch a hole in the center of the rubber using an awl. Attach the base and wire cover using a nut and bolt suitable for the size of the hole, along with washers to hold everything together securely.

Tip Make sure the objects you choose are able to hold the weight of what you want to put in them. Be careful to balance the object on the base securely. Screw-in door handles or pot handles are good, and make an unusual object.

Found Object Fruit Bowls

Wok Lid Bowl

1. This fruit bowl started life as a lid for a wok. The base is an old stainless steel toilet roll holder with an attached pole.

2. Remove the handle from the wok lid, turn it around to the inside of the wok lid, and attach it to the base. This fruit bowl uses the knob from an old pressure cooker but you can use whatever you have lying about, even a door handle.

Tip To attach together items that have holes in the middle that are bigger then a typical screw head, use a fender washer on either side of the assembly to pinch the pieces together. Fender washers have a large outside diameter but a small inside diameter, and can bridge across a large hole. If an especially large washer is needed, create one by scrounging the lid of a metal tin or other container and drilling a hole in the center.

Zen Bamboo Lamp

Time: 🕐   **Skill:** ⟍⟍

Materials

- Old bamboo place mat
- 2 bamboo trivets
- Scrap of old fabric
- Metal strip with a hole in it to fit across the trivet
- Board pin or thumbtack
- Two small angle brackets
- Small piece of perforated metal sheet or thin plywood cut to size
- Needle and thread
- Screws, nuts, and bolts
- Adhesive spray or glue

see over for tools . . .

Old bamboo place mats, combined with a bamboo trivet, make fantastic lamp shades as they filter the light in an interesting way. The trivets form the base and top of the light, while the place mat creates the lamp shade.

1. Measure around the inside of the trivet.

2. Cut the place mat across its length to the same size as the inside measurement of the trivet. The width of the mat forms the height of the lamp.

3. Glue the fabric to the mat to give the lamp its lining. Here a piece of material from an old blind was used. White fabrics work best as they diffuse the light.

4. Using the needle and thread, stitch the two edges of the mat to form a cylinder. Use simple straight stitches about 2" apart. For the most attractive result, the thread should match the color of the placemat. After the first few stitches, check that the completed cylinder fits the inside measurements of the trivet.

5. Secure the lined placemat to one of the trivets using a board pin. This will form the base of the lamp. Secure the second trivet to the other end of the mat to form the top.

6. Mark a point on the inside of each face of the lamp ½" from the top and bottom edge. Use the awl to make a hole at this point.

107

Tools

- Awl
- Handsaw
- Drill

7. Secure the mat to the inside of the trivets using small screws.

8. Using a handsaw, cut a square piece of wood sized to slip inside the base of the lamp. Drill a $\frac{1}{2}$" diameter hole in the center of the square and glue the strips to the bottom of the square along opposite sides. This should give you someting that looks like a little table with a hole in the middle. Glue it into the bottom of the lamp shade with the "legs" facing down.

9. Follow the instructions on page 38 to wire the lamp. Thread a 1 $\frac{1}{4}$" piece of lamp rod into the base of the socket.

10. Lastly, put the end of the cord through the hole in the base of tthe lamp, insert the rod through the hole, thread a nut onto the end and then install a plug on the end of the cord. Remember: When you turn it on for the first time keep an eye on the shade to make sure it stays cool enough, and use a small low wattage bulb to avoid overheating the shade.

Tip Two identical wooden picture frames (without glass) would make a good substitute for the trivets. Or you could scrounge some wood to make a pair of simple wood frames. You could also try following the wood bending instructions on page 90 to make a pair of matching wood rings rather than squares, which would create a round lamp. An old wooden blind could be trimmed and used to make the lamp shade instead of the place mat.

Record Album Mail Organizer

Time: 🕐 **Skill:** ⟑⟑

Materials

- 4–6 record albums
- Small grommets or rivets

Tools

- Iron and ironing board
- Old T-shirt
- Gloves
- Cardboard or wooden tube such as packaging roll or small rolling pin, 1½" in diameter, at least 18" long
- Grommet tool
- Spring clamps or binder clips

It's easy to find some really awful record albums at garage sales and thrift stores. Changes in technology aside, their content alone is reason enough to assume that they'll never be played again. So why not sacrifice a few in the name of home décor?

The first step is to bend the records. The organizer in the photo uses four records. You'll need a couple of extra ones for practice first, though.

1. Heat the iron to "high." Slip the record inside an old T-shirt and place it on the ironing board. Run the iron over the T-shirt and record for 20–30 seconds, moving it slowly the entire time. Focus on a line tangent to the record's label. The goal is to soften this area enough to allow it to bend while leaving the rest of the disk stiff and flat.

2. When the time is up, put on the gloves, as the record will be very hot. Quickly pull the record out of the shirt and wrap the softened area around the tube to form it into a "U" shape.

3. When you have four nicely bent records, stack them as shown in the photo and use three grommets or rivets to join each album to its neighbor.

4. Once they are all fastened together, hang the unit on a nail in the wall, using the spindle hole of the top record. Now you have a hip organizer for sorting your mail and you never need to listen to those ghastly old records again.

Tin Can Pen Rack

Time: 🕐   **Skill:** ↖

Materials

- Aluminum rod, ½" in diameter, 24" long
- 5 identical cans
- Thick black hair elastics (buy the longest ones you can find)
- Pushpins (long length and with aluminum heads work best) or nails

Tools

- Tubing cutter or hacksaw
- Steel wool

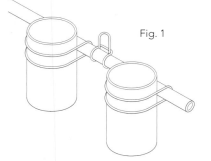

Fig. 1

If you peel away the label and objectively consider the common can, the ribbed, polished surface is actually rather pleasing.

This is one of the simplest projects in the book. If you already have a dowel or rod the right length, no tools are required. A ½" diameter aluminum tube is pictured, but any stiff rod, tube, dowel, or even a reasonably straight stick of roughly the same diameter will do the job.

1. Use the tubing cutter, cut the aluminum tube to length. (A hacksaw will also work, but you'll have to file the cut ends to remove any burrs. The tubing cutter does a quicker, cleaner job.)

2. Buff the surface of the rod with the steel wool for a nice shine.

3. Clean the cans well and remove the labels and glue. Stubborn glue can be removed with a bit of WD-40 or other solvent.

4. Loop the elastics around the cans and the tube as shown in Fig. 1. The elastics should rest in the ribs of the cans.

5. Loop two more elastics around the rod to use as hanging points.

6. Push two pushpins or hammer two fine nails into your wall far enough apart to line up with the hanging loops.

7. Hang the assembly on the pins and fill the cans with your pens, pencils, markers, and whatever else will relieve the clutter on your desk. You can even insert a note, photo, or sheet of paper between the wall and the bottom edges of the cans, which will stay in place by friction alone.

CD Case Photo Display

Materials

- 2 aluminum channels, 4 ft long with an inside width of ½"
- Heavyweight illustration board
- CD cases
- Photos, found art, news clippings, colored paper
- 3 flathead wire nails

Tools

- Tape measure
- Hacksaw
- Fine file
- Straightedge
- Pencil
- Utility knife
- Steel wool
- Silicone sealant
- Caulk gun
- Hammer

No one has a shortage of CD cases after converting their music to MP3 format. And it seems such a shame to throw them out. This project puts them to use in an easily changeable, modular photo display.

Vary the look by adding colored paper or found art rather than just photographs. The example opposite is 4 ft long; a longer version would be a great way to dress up a hallway and an excellent way to display many of your favorite snapshots or trimmed postcards.

1. Take an extra piece of the aluminum channel and a CD case with you when you buy the illustration board. Choose board thick enough to fit snugly into the channel behind the case yet thin enough still to allow the cases to slide out. See Fig.1a and 1b, on the next page, for how the three materials should fit together.

2. Cut the channels to the desired length. Use a file to remove any burrs from the cuts and buff with steel wool until the aluminum shines.

3. Use the utility knife and straightedge to cut the illustration board into sufficient strips to give a length that is 8" shorter than the channels and ⅛" wider than the CD cases. Line them up end to end.

4. Run a bead of silicone along the inside edge of the channels. (The stuff you use to caulk around your bathtub is fine.) Slip the edges of the board into the channels and press them down into the sealant.

CD Case Photo Display

Fig. 1a

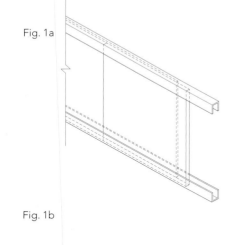

Fig. 1b

5. Once the board is in place and the ends of the channels line up with each other, slide the CD cases into the channels to ensure the board is bedded well in the silicone. The cases will wedge things in place as the silicone cures. Make sure no excess silicone is oozing out and gluing the cases in place.

6. Prepare the artwork and trim it to size. Pop the CD cases apart and remove the insert that clips the CD in place. Insert the artwork into the back face of the case, then reinstall the insert and the cover.

7. When the silicone is cured, hang the frame on the wall by nailing through the illustration board. Slip the CD cases into the ends of the channels.

Slate Tile Mirror

Time: 🕐 **Skill:** ⚒

Materials

- Offcut of slate
- Mirror
- Picture hook and nail
- Tacks
- Felt

see over for tools . . .

Old mirrors are a perennial find at garage sales, flea markets, thrift shops and so on, but a lot of them have ugly, old-fashioned frames that don't fit well with contemporary design. However, this shouldn't prevent you from reusing the perfectly good mirror by reframing it with an alternative. Here, an offcut of slate from a tiling company was used to create a stylish new mirror.

If you have the slate but no mirror, this can be purchased inexpensively from a glass store, but it's also simple to trim a smaller piece out of a broken mirror that has been discarded. A glasscutter, some oil to lubricate the cutter wheel, and a straightedge are all the tools that are necessary.

1. Use the square, straightedge, and marker pen to draw the cut marks on the piece of slate. Remember that the hole in the frame should be slightly smaller than the size of the mirror. Using the sharp point of a tile cutter, score the surface as deeply as possible. Then, with bevelled side down, use a bricklayer's trowel to chop the edge.

2. If you need to cut the mirror to size, use the square, straightedge, and marker pen to lay out the cut marks on the mirror so that the trimmed piece will fit into the frame with just a little room to spare. Cut the mirror or board with the glasscutter or saw, insert it into the frame, and press some map pins into the frame behind it to hold everything in place.

117

Slate Tile Mirror

Tools

- Fine-tip marker pen
- Square
- Straightedge
- Tile cutter
- Trowel
- Glasscutter
- Household oil
- Handsaw or circular saw
- Hammer
- Map pins

3. As the wheel of the cutter is rolled along the straightedge, it etches a line in the surface of the glass, weakening it at that point. The scored line is then aligned with a table edge and flexed. With a bit of luck, the glass should break cleanly along the line you just scored. (Note that glass dust is created when glass is etched and it's good to have a damp paper towel handy to wipe it up.)

4. Back the mirror with some cardboard and then cut a piece of strong cloth such as felt to slightly larger than the size of the mirror. Glue the felt to the slate frame to hold the mirror in place.

Variation: Slate Place Settings

If you have scraps of slate that aren't large enough to make a frame, use them to create personalized place settings for your dinner parties. Either cut the pieces of slate to the required size using the technique in step 1, or leave them as you found them for a more interesting shape. Write the names of your guests on the slate in chalk before you set the table. You could even write out the whole menu so your guests know what they have to look forward to. And the best bit? They're totally recyclable—simply wipe clean ready for your next party.

Tip You can also use the slate to make a stylish picture frame, or anything else that springs to mind. Or you can use a different kind of tile—it doesn't have to be slate.

Carry Along Cushions

Time: 🕐   **Skill:** ↖

Materials

- Rice sack
- Old cushion

Tools

- Scissors
- Needle and thread

Empty rice sacks can easily be turned into cushions that will really brighten up your sofa or garden chairs. Alternatively, the handles on the bag mean you can carry the cushion around with you to picnics or to the beach. You can even take the cushion out and fill the bag up with shells, stones, or anything else you want to collect while you're out and about.

No-Sew Version

1. Take an empty rice sack and the cushion pad out of an old cushion or pillow that you don't use any more.

2. Push the cushion inside the bag. If the bag has a zip, as with the white cushion, all you need to do is zip the bag up and your cushion is ready to go.

Needle and Thread Version

1. If your rice sack doesn't have a zip, as in the yellow cushion, you can sew the top of the bag shut.

2. Alternatively, make a cut in the center of each of the handles. Then tie the two sides of the cushion together using the handles. A bow looks prettier, but you can use a knot if the handles are too short.

Tip If you want to make a waterproof cover for cushions you can use in the garden, use one of the bigger, waterproof sacks or bags on the market. Some of them have interesting colors and text, ranging from advertisements to film posters.

Decoupage Tray

Materials

- Printers' tray
- Text or image to lay over the tray
- Felt or plastic backing

Tools

- Fine grade sandpaper or wet and dry sandpaper
- Plastic wood or putty
- Acrylic primer
- Paint
- Fixative such as glue
- Gold leaf
- Varnish

Decoupage is the process of finishing or decorating an object by gluing colored or printed paper to it and then applying coats of a clear sealer until the surface feels smooth. In this case we've brought to life an old printers' trays from a flea market, but the same technique can be applied to larger items such as old bland furniture.

The inspiration for using the script came from the fact that the tray was originally used to store metal types and fonts for printing. The paper you use in your project can also play on the item's former life, or not. Be creative!

1. Remove any knobs or buttons from the tray. Clean the tray thoroughly and, when it is dry, smooth and sand it.

2. Fill any holes with plastic wood or putty and sand the tray again to create a smooth surface.

3. Prepare the tray using an acrylic primer.

4. Paint a base coat of red acrylic paint and leave to dry, then apply another coat.

5. There are many ways of finishing the tray. To copy the script tray, enlarge and photocopy in black and white a page of script slightly smaller than the tray, leaving a ½" red border when you glue the paper to the tray.

6. Brush a used tea bag over the photocopy to give it an aged look and allow it to dry, then use a fixative spray to seal the image.

7. Place gold leaf randomly over the script and the edges of the tray.

8. Apply 5–6 coats of matte water-based acrylic varnish to the entire tray, alternating the direction of strokes on each layer.

9. Sand with fine grade sandpaper or wet and dry sandpaper after the first three coats and before the last coat of varnish, wiping with a dry cloth after each sanding. Leave the varnish to dry thoroughly before applying each layer of varnish. Seal the piece with a last coat of varnish.

10. To finish the tray, cut a piece of felt or cloth the same size as the tray and fix it to the bottom of the tray. In this case plastic backing, which was originally from a rice sack, was used. A roll of 1" cork strip found in a scrap bank was then glued onto the tray to form a border. Felt can be used instead of cork.

Variation: Decoupage Table Top

Use the same technique to create a stunning table top, following the same technique as for the tray.

Tip Any kind of image, text, or print could be used to finish the tray, including newspaper, notepaper, or magazines. Instead of using a cloth or plastic backing for the underside you can use a primer and two coats of acrylic paint. Four felt pads can be fixed to the four corners to protect the table surface. In a similar way, drawers from old tables and kitchen units—or old trays—can be given a quick and dramatic facelift.

Slide Show Light Feature

Materials

- Cable junction box
- $\frac{3}{32}$" x 3" wide wood sheets (available at craft and hobby stores)
- Scrap cardboard or mat board
- Slides
- 2 scrap wood blocks
- Nuts and bolts
- Slim fluorescent strip light
- Scrap plexiglass

Tools

- Electric drill
- Gel-type Krazy glue
- Utlity knife
- Pencil
- Straightedge
- Plexiglass knife

Time: 🕐 **Skill:** ↖

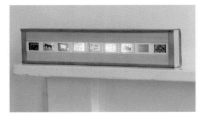

You can make interesting objects from bits of architectural salvage, for instance, an electrical panel or cable junction box, which are often discarded when offices renovate. They are used to hide cables along the walls of buildings, but you can use a box and some old slides to make a great light feature.

Use pictures of your family, holiday, or anything you find interesting. It is designed to be easily taken apart, so you can change the images to keep things interesting—or to redecorate your home.

1. Clean the cable junction box thoroughly. Drill two holes in the back of the junction box to correspond to the holes in the strip light housing.

2. Cut two wood blocks to fit snugly into the ends of the junction box while leaving a $\frac{3}{8}$" gap between the block and the back of the box for air circulation.

3. Fit the blocks to the ends of the box and measure the space between them. This is the space you have available to display your slides.

4. Cut two pieces from the wood sheet with a utility knife. The measurements are determined as follows: First measure the height of the slides and the width of the junction box. Subtract the height of the slides from the width of the junction box and divide the result by two. Add $\frac{1}{4}$" to allow for some overlap.

5. Cut two more strips from from thin wood or cardboard, using the same length measurement as before but $\frac{1}{4}$" narrower. Make sure the wood or cardboard is at least as thick as the slides.

125

6. Cut a piece of transparent plexiglass (⅛" thick minimum) to match the inside width of the box. The length should match the length of the wood strips you just cut.

7. Glue the narrower slats to the face of the plexiglass, one along the top edge and one along the bottom. Make sure the slides fit between the two strips before the glue dries. Then glue the wider strips to the tops of the narrow strips, again aligning the edges.

8. Glue one block into the end of the junction box to prevent the slides from falling out.

9. Insert the plastic and wood panel into the box and hold it tight against the lips along the top and bottom edges of the box. Inside the top and bottom of the box, glue strips of wood in place to hold the panel against the lips. Take care not to accidentally glue the panel into place as well. You want to be able to slide it out to change the lightbulb.

10. Attach the strip light in place.

11. To finish, slot your slides into place in front of the plexiglass. Insert the remaining wood block in the open end of the box and turn the light on.

Tip If you don't have a cable junction box, you could use some other architectural salvage such as metal wall studs or gutters. And instead of using store-bought wood, consider using the slats from a discarded wooden window blind, as we used here.

Candy-Wrapper Bowl

Time: ◑ **Skill:** ↖

Materials

- Candy wrappers

Tools

- Needle and thread

Collect the foil coverings of chocolate and candy wrappers and use them to create a shimmering bowl.

1. Start by twisting one foil wrapper into a tight roll. Connect the next wrapper to it by twisting the ends together to create a rope.

2. When the candy-wrapper rope is about 2 ft long, form one end into a small circle. Using a needle and some strong thread (you could cut a long thin strip from a plastic bag), stitch the circle together.

3. Next, create a second candy-wrapper rope about 10 ft long and start attaching it to the inner circle. Secure each stitch by looping the thread around the needle and pulling it. Use simple stitches (or a blanket stitch) and form a tight spiral, coiling the foil rope to create a bowl shape.

4. Attach two rows of coils of the same size to the bottom of the bowl to make a stand.

Variation: Plastic Bag Coasters

Use the same technique to create colorful coasters out of plastic bags. Twist the bags together using the same technique as for the foil wrappers, making sure to use a variety of different colors, and stitch together to form a circle. The advantage of using plastic bags is that the coasters will be waterproof, so you won't ruin them if you spill your drink.

Night Stand

Time: 🌓   **Skill:** ʅʅʅ

Materials

- 1 piece of wood 1" x 4" and 4 ft long (or 4 scraps at least 12" long)
- 1 cutting board, wood or plastic, at least 14" x 15"
- ⅛" thick clear plexiglass at least 13" x 14"
- Mat board at least 12" x 12"
- 1 piano hinge 12" long with screws
- 2 self-adhesive furniture feet ⅛" thick
- 2 high-strength magnets (from stationery store)
- 2 keyhole hooks
- 4 shelf pins
- 8 screws 1½" long min
- 4 screws ⅜" long max
- Wood glue

    see over for tools . . .

By day, these little drop-front cabinets appear to be simple photo frames. But at night they open to serve as bedside tables. In other situations, they could also work as end tables or, turn one 90 degrees and use it as a key cabinet near your entry.

These tables are not very large: 16" by 16" is about a big as you want to go to avoid overstressing the hinge. The 1 x 4 lumber used here is 3½" wide and will make a cabinet deep enough to hold a Kleenex tissue box lying on its side. Other than that, the dimensions are flexible and may be adjusted based on the materials available.

1. Cut two pieces of wood 9½" long for the top and bottom and two pieces 12" long for the sides.

2. Drill a pair of holes part way through each side to accommodate the shelf pins. Alternatively, glue on two slim strips of wood or metal to support the shelf.

3. Arrange the top and bottom pieces between the sides to form a rectangular box

4. We used a plate joiner to make a concealed connection at each of the corners, but using a pair of screws to join each corner will work just as well. Just remember to pre-drill the screw hole to prevent the wood from splitting. In any case, be sure to use some sort of mechanical connection here for strength. Don't rely on wood glue alone.

5. Once the wood pieces are joined, you have the frame of your cabinet and it's time to install the keyhole hooks. These hooks will slide over the head of a screw in the wall and drop down over it,

Tools

- Electric drill
- Variety of drill bits
- Scrap wood to put under work-piece when drilling
- Sandpaper
- Circular saw
- Plexiglass knife
- File
- Hacksaw
- Pencil
- Tape measure
- Square
- Utility knife
- Straightedge
- Small and large screwdrivers

securely holding the cabinet in place. Before you attach the hook plate to the cabinet, drill out some wood beneath it to provide clearance for the screw head. You can then put the plate on. Locate it about quarter of the way from the top of the cabinet.

6. If you plan to paint or clear-coat the cabinet, do so now.

7. Cut the mat board to a size large enough to cover the back of the cabinet. The hooks will prevent the mat from lying flat on the wood, so cut notches in the sides of the mat to clear them. Once it fits nicely, glue the mat to the back of the cabinet frame.

8. If necessary, trim the cutting board to size. Ideally, it should overlap the cabinet by 1" or so on the top and sides and 3" at the bottom. The 3" overlap at the bottom helps to support the tabletop when it is in the down position. If you trim a plastic cutting board, use a file to smooth the cut edges.

9. Using the plexiglass knife, cut the plexi to a size a bit smaller than the final dimensions of the cutting board.

10. While your tools are out, cut a piece of plexi or one of the cutting board scraps to use as a shelf in the cabinet.

11. On the cutting board, draw a line 3" from one of the short edges. Line the barrel of the hinge up with this mark with the leaves pointing toward the edge you measured from. Screw the hinge in place using all of the screw holes available. To get a hinge the right length, you may have to use a hacksaw to cut a longer hinge down to size. If so, locate your cuts to maximize the number of screw holes in the leaves of the hinge.

12. Place the cutting board over the face of the cabinet and unfold the hinge so that the free leaf is against the bottom of the cabinet. Then screw that leaf in place.

13. Stick two rubber furniture pads to the bottom of the cabinet. These will act as shims to keep the tabletop level when it is in the down position.

14. With the cutting board/tabletop in the closed position, center the plexiglass on the surface that will be the underside of the table. Drill four holes through the plexi into the cutting board. Put your photo under the plexi and screw it in place using the holes you just drilled.

15. To make a catch to hold the cutting board in the closed position, use a pair of magnets. Flip the tabletop open and drill a hole in the face of the top of the cabinet. Glue one of the magnets into the hole. Locate the matching spot on the tabletop and do the same for the second magnet. Before you glue it in though, make sure its polarity is facing the right way!

16. To hang the nightstand, measure the distance between the centers of the keyhole hooks and mark those locations on the wall. Install two screws in the wall that have heads small enough to fit into the hooks. Be sure to use wall anchors to prevent the screws from pulling out of the wall.

17. When your project is mounted, set the shelf in place. Stand back, admire your work, and go stock up your night stand with whatever you need for the night!

Techniques

Drilling Holes

GENERAL RULES
- Wear eye protection. Make sure hair, clothing, and jewelry are pulled back and secured to avoid snagging or tangling.
- Don't advance the bit too quickly. When drilling hard or brittle material like plastic, it is helpful to start the hole with a small bit and work up to the final size bit.
- Drill bits can get hot during drilling, especially if they are dull or if you are making a large hole. Back the drill out of the hole periodically to help eject shavings and allow the bit to cool.

1. First, mark the location of the hole on your work piece. If you have multiple holes to make, it is most efficient to do all the layout work at once.

2. Use an awl or center punch to mark the center of the hole. This makes a little divot for the tip of the drill bit to rest in, which helps keep it accurately located and prevents it slipping to the side as you begin to drill.

3. If the work piece is small, clamp it to the bench top or hold it securely in a vise. If you intend to drill all of the way through the material, place a piece of scrap wood beneath the hole to avoid drilling into the bench. This will also prevent your work piece from splintering (see Fig. 1).

4. Select a drill and bit based on the size and depth of the hole and the material you'll be drilling into. Insert the bit into the chuck of the drill and tighten it so that the bit is held securely.

5. Place the tip of the drill bit on the center mark that you made with the awl and hold the drill so the bit is perpendicular to the work surface. From whatever direction you look at it, it should not look tipped. If it does, the hole will be made through the work piece at a skewed angle (see Fig. 2).

6. Most electric drills have a variable speed trigger which works like the gas pedal on a car— the harder you press, the faster it goes. As you start drilling, the motor should run relatively slowly. Once the hole is established, you can increase the speed. When the hole reaches full depth, keep the motor running and pull the bit from the hole. Don't stop the drill with the bit in the hole—it may bind, and be tough to remove.

With that, the hole is complete.

Fig. 1

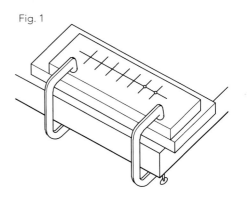

Fig. 2

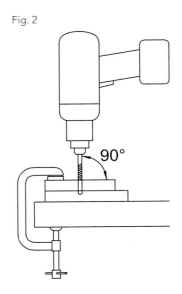

Clamping/Holding

Without a sturdy base on which to work and a secure means to hold a piece of work, it is difficult to obtain the best results. To avoid frustration and for safety's sake, it is important to support a work piece during each step of fabrication, repair, or assembly.

GENERAL RULES
- Ensure the work piece will be adequately supported throughout the entire process.
- Keep clamping surfaces clear and clean, as debris can damage the surface of a work piece.
- Place scraps of wood between the work and the jaws of a clamp or vise to distribute the pressure and to avoid scratching, denting, or discoloring the work piece.
- Assemble your project beforehand without the use of glue or fasteners, to ensure all the pieces fit properly. Use this opportunity to decide how many clamps you willl need and where they will be positioned.
- Arrange the clamps on the work piece to apply pressure evenly.
- Do not use a clamp or vise to force objects together. If they do not mate properly, find out why and correct the problem.

Clamps are available for almost any size project. Below is a brief overview of the common types (see Fig. 1 and 2):

SPRING CLAMPS
These work like large clothes pins. They don't exert much pressure, but can be applied and removed quickly using only one hand.

C-CLAMPS
Many different sized C-clamps are available, but those between 1 and 6 inches are most common. Their strong, rigid frames mean they can deliver a large amount of pressure to a small area.

PARALLEL JAW CLAMPS
The broad surface area of their jaws distributes pressure more evenly and that, combined with their wooden jaws, makes them less likely to dent or mar a woodwork piece.

BAR CLAMPS
These are used for clamping larger projects like drawers or boxes. Their maximum capacity depends on the length of the bar. Clamps with bars from 6" to 36" long are available.

PIPE CLAMPS
Pipe clamps are similar to bar clamps except that they can be made much longer (up to several feet) since they use stiff steel pipe as the "bar." The clamping mechanism will also deliver more pressure than the smaller, lighter bar clamps. This makes pipe clamps suitable for very large projects such as furniture and cabinetry.

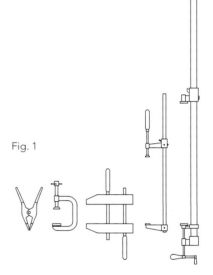

Fig. 1

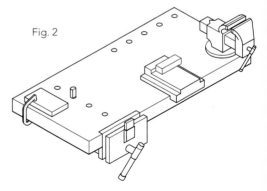

Fig. 2

Using a Glasscutter

A glasscutter doesn't really cut the glass. It just scores the surface so that you can break it in a controlled way. The glass will tend to fracture along the line of weakness created by the score, which is created by drawing the cutter across the glass along a straightedge, as you would when cutting something with a utility knife.

GENERAL RULES
- When the cutter rolls across the glass, it leaves a trail of glass dust behind. Have a damp paper towel on hand to wipe this up.
- Work on top of some sheets of newspaper to catch any stray glass splinters.
- Wear eye protection when scoring and snapping the glass.

First you need to do some prep work. Clean the glass well and make sure it is free of grease, and lubricate the cutting wheel well so that it rolls, rather than slides, on the glass. When you use the cutter, expect to hear a grinding noise.

Use your straightedge to mark where you need to score. Score the full width of the glass and lighten your pressure as you reach the end of the cut so you don't chip the edge.

Flip the glass over and use the ball on the end of the cutter to gently tap the glass behind the score to weaken it. Flip the glass back over, align the score with a table edge or with a strip of wood on the table top, and flex the glass. The glass should break along the score line. If the break isn't straight, hook one of the notches in the cutter over the remaining bits to nibble them back to the score line. An oilstone can be used to dull the sharp edge of the glass.

Scoring Cardboard

When you score, cut the cardboard but don't go all the way through so the skin of one side of the cardboard acts as a hinge. Practice on some scrap pieces first to get a feel for how deep you need to cut to score rather than sever right through.

Cutting with Blades

The quickest and cleanest way to cut many thin materials is with a knife, rather than with scissors or some type of saw. In each situation, the same basic techniques apply. First, a few words about the tools available.

Hobby knives generally have small pointed blades that clamp into pen-like handles. These are best reserved for fine-scale or detail-oriented work. Longer cuts and thicker materials are usually better dealt with by utility knives, of which there are two basic types. Sheet rock knives have replaceable trapezoid-shaped blades that are stiff and strong, which makes them suitable for heavy-duty cutting. The other type has a long blade housed in the handle that can be advanced and broken off in increments as the tip dulls. These make good all-purpose knives and will work well for most of the projects in the book that call for a knife.

Rotary cutters are used in a manner similar to knives, but rather than dragging the edge of a blade across a surface, the cutter has a round blade that rolls across. These are very sharp and can only be used to cut fabric and paper, but do an excellent job at it.

Long, straight cuts are best accomplished by cutting along a straightedge. Steel, aluminum, and plastic straightedges are available. The best general-purpose edge is a cork-backed steel ruler. The cork helps prevent the ruler from slipping during the cut and the knife will not dig into the steel, which can occur with aluminum or plastic straightedges if they are not used carefully. In fact, plastic straightedges are generally to be used only with rotary cutters.

Also, something should be placed beneath the cut to avoid marring the work surface. Scrap cardboard will work in a pinch, but purchasing a self-healing cutting mat from a craft store is a wise investment. It's cheaper than a new dining room table…

GENERAL RULES
- Measure out where the cut needs to occur, then set the material on the cutting mat, making sure the cut won't run beyond the mat.
- Align the straightedge with the marks and hold it firmly in place, keeping your fingers well away from the edge along which the knife will travel.
- Act out the cut beforehand, making sure nothing important is in the way if the knife were to slip.
- Draw the knife along the edge with a medium pressure. It's better to make a few passes with the knife than try to cut all the way through in one shot.

Using Tin Snips

Tin snips are large, heavy-duty scissors with short, deep cutting edges. They are available in lengths ranging from 7" to 16". There are three types of tin snips, distinguished by colored handles. Yellow indicates a shear capable of making a straight-ahead cut, and cuts to the right or left; red indicates a straight-ahead cut, or a cut curved to the left; green indicates a straight-ahead cut, or a cut curved to the right. Red- and green-handled shears can cut tighter curves than yellow-handled types.

GENERAL RULES
- Long handles give good leverage to cut through thick materials.
- For more control, you can clamp one handle of the snips in a bench vise, allowing you to concentrate on guiding the material through the shears.
- When buying these tools, look for smoothly operating shears that have well-forged components.
- You can sharpen a used pair of tin snips by clamping them in a vise and filing the edge to an 85° angle.

To cut a tight outside curve or circle with straight-bladed shears or snips, nibble away until you achieve the shape you need.

Keep the cutting edge of the tool perpendicular to the sheet metal, otherwise the tool can slip sideways and wedge between the cutting jaws, fouling the work and the tool.

Resources

www.mcmaster.com
An industrial supply house that stocks so much stuff you could probably build your own space station and furnish it. It's a good place to look for unusual hardware and is chockful of informative little primers on various products and materials.

www.freecycle.org
Rather than putting usable items in the trash, people post them here to give other people a chance to claim and use them.

www.rockler.com
A broad selection of woodworking tools and unusual hardware.

www.sciplus.com
American Science and Surplus with lots of odd surplus goodies for inspiration.

www.craigslist.com
Free online want ads.

www.readymademag.com
A great magazine for people who like to make stuff.

www.makezine.com
Make Magazine's online version with forums, projects, a store, and blogs.

Index

Index

TIME

A YEAR IN SPACE

INSIDE SCOTT KELLY'S HISTORIC MISSION—
IS TRAVEL TO MARS NEXT?

◀ **The International Space Station** holds more than an acre of solar panels, weighs close to a million pounds and carries close to seven tons of supplies.

// THE SPACE-TIME CONTINUUM

SPACE TRAVEL LOOKS LIKE FUN—WHAT with weightlessness and the views— but it can be hard on the human body. In the absence of gravity, muscles, bones, the heart and even the eyes can suffer damage. That's why it's so remarkable that astronaut Scott Kelly and cosmonaut Mikhail Kornienko spent a year aboard the International Space Station to help run the biomedical studies that will help determine whether humans are capable of making a two-and-a-half-year journey to Mars.

TIME has covered their marathon mission in the magazine and in a yearlong video series called *A Year in Space*, the basis for a one-hour TIME and PBS documentary in 2016 and a planned sequel in 2017. TIME editor at large Jeffrey Kluger and TIME Video supervising producer Jonathan Woods, working with

director Shaul Schwarz and co-director Marco Grob, followed Scott's preparation for his takeoff in March 2015 and his experiences in orbit. Scott's identical twin brother Mark, a retired astronaut, served as a perfect control subject for the year-in-space study—a man with a genetic template identical to Scott's, who spent a year growing older on Earth while his brother grew older in space. "The twins study was too serendipitous an opportunity for NASA to pass up," says Kluger.

It makes for good storytelling too. "We've been trusted to have our cameras in places they don't usually go," says Woods, "and what we deliver based on that trust is a rare first account of an unprecedented mission." Watch our video series at time.com/space. For information on viewing the full-length documentary, go to pbs.org/yearinspace

Nancy Gibbs

—Nancy Gibbs, Editor of TIME

CONTENTS

ABOUT THE AUTHOR

Jeffrey Kluger is editor at large for TIME magazine and Time.com and an executive producer of the documentary series *A Year in Space*. He is the author of nine books, including *Apollo 13*, on which the 1995 movie was based, and two novels for young adults.

◄ This picture of an aurora was tweeted by astronaut Scott Kelly as he passed over Earth in August 2015.

Parts of this edition appeared previously in TIME and on Time.com.

// BLASTING INTO THE FUTURE

NASA'S GRAND PLAN TO REACH MARS INVOLVES A REMARKABLE EXPERIMENT, TWIN ASTRONAUTS AND 5,440 ORBITS AROUND EARTH

Before his launch, astronaut Scott Kelly sits inside a Soyuz simulator at the Gagarin Cosmonaut Training Center in March 2015.

WHEN SCOTT KELLY CALLED HOME from the International Space Station (ISS) before his reentry on March 2, he knew that whoever answered the phone might simply hang up on him. The calls were welcome, but the link could be lousy, with long, hissing silences breaking up the conversation. That's what happens when you're placing your call from 250 miles above Earth while zipping along at 17,150 miles per hour and your signal has to get bounced from satellites to ground antennas to relay stations like an around-the-horn triple play. "When someone answers, I have to say, 'It's the space station! Don't hang up!'" said Kelly before he left Earth.

That wasn't necessary when he called his brother Mark. Perhaps best known as the husband of former congresswoman Gabrielle Giffords, who was grievously wounded in an assassination attempt in 2011, Mark is a former astronaut who has been to space four times. He knows the crackle of an extraterrestrial signal in his ear, just as he knows the singular feeling of weightlessness, the singular sweep of Earth outside the window—and the power of 250 miles of altitude to make a person feel alone. Drive that in the flat and it's nothing more than Syracuse to Boston. Fly it straight up and it's a whole other thing.

But most of all, Mark, 52, knows Scott, 52—which is how it is with brothers, especially when they're identical twins, born factory-loaded with the exact same genetic operating system. The brothers' connection was more important than ever in March 2015, when Scott took off for his one-year stay aboard the space station, setting a single-mission record for a U.S. astronaut.

Scott was partnered in his marathon mission with Russian cosmonaut Mikhail ("Misha") Kornienko. They, in turn, were joined by a rotating cast of 13 other crew members, all of whom were aboard for anywhere from 10 days to six months, conducting experiments and reconfiguring various station modules for the arrival of privately built crew vehicles, which could come as early as 2017.

A year in space required Scott to leave behind a lot: his Houston home, his daughters—Samantha, 21, and Charlotte, 12—and his girlfriend of six years, Amiko Kauderer, a NASA public-affairs officer. (He and his first wife are divorced.) But in some ways, he didn't leave Mark behind.

Ever since the Apollo days, the U.S. has vaguely discussed a crewed mission to Mars, though the target date for the grand expedition has always remained a convenient decade or two away. But on Dec. 5, 2014, NASA took a big step toward that goal with the successful uncrewed test flight of the Apollo-like Orion spacecraft, America's deep-space ship of the future. Add to that the competition from upstarts like Elon Musk's SpaceX and nations like China and India, with their own surging space programs, and the scramble for cosmic supremacy is accelerating fast.

The biggest problem with our exploratory ambitions is, simply, us. The human body is a purpose-built machine, designed for the one-G environment of Earth. Take us into the zero-G of space or the 0.38-G of Mars and it all comes unsprung. Bones get brittle, eyeballs lose their shape, hearts beat less efficiently since they no longer have to pump against gravity, and balance goes awry. At least that's what we know so far. "There's quite a bit of data [on human health] for six months in orbit," says former space-station program manager Mike Suffredini. "But have we reached stasis at six months, or do things change at one year? Is there a knee in the curve we haven't reached yet?"

So NASA needs subjects to venture out and run the long-duration tests. In a perfect experiment, every one of those subjects would also have a control subject on the ground—someone with, say, the exact same genes and a very similar temperament, so you could tease apart

> "WHEN SOMEONE ANSWERS, I HAVE TO SAY, 'IT'S THE SPACE STATION! DON'T HANG UP!'"
> —SCOTT KELLY

▲ Mark (left) and Scott Kelly talk to reporters in January 2015 about Scott's one-year mission.

the changes that come from being aloft for 12 months from those that are a result of growing the same year older on Earth. In the Kelly brothers, NASA has that two-person sample group. "The twins study didn't come up when we were selecting crew for the mission," says Suffredini. "But it occurred to us later that we had this ground-based truth in Mark."

What NASA calls a "ground-based truth," of course, Scott calls a big brother (by six minutes). And while the mission that concluded on March 2, 2016, was equal parts science experiment, endurance test and human drama, it was to the Kelly brothers (and only the Kelly brothers) just the latest mile in a journey they've shared for half a century.

ROCKET MEN

It's a matter of historical record that Scott and Mark Kelly never got around to building an airplane. They never built a rocket ship either, but on both counts they can be forgiven. There's rarely much follow-through when you're 5 years old and you hatch your plans at night, in whispers, after your parents have put you to bed.

The brothers did their planning around the time of the Apollo 11 moon landing, when space travel seemed sublimely cool. They were alike in their fascination with space—and in other ways. Like many twins, they spoke their own private language in toddlerhood, gibberish that was unintelligible to adults but seemed to make perfect sense to them. They dressed alike until first grade too. "There is a picture of us in orange shorts, orange striped shirts and bow ties," Mark says with a small wince. "We did everything together until college and were always on the edge of getting into trouble."

By the late 1980s, both brothers were commissioned as naval aviators, and they were assigned to active duty aboard aircraft carriers. Upon finishing their first squadron assignment and tour of duty, both became Navy test pilots. In 1995 they applied to NASA, and by 1996, they were dressing identically once again—and once again in orange—this time in the pressure suits of a space-shuttle astronaut.

From 1999 on, the brothers served a combined eight missions, though they never went to space together. (NASA had no

▲ Mere weeks before liftoff, Mikhail Kornienko (left), Gennady Padalka (center) and Scott Kelly sit outside a Soyuz simulator in Star City, Russia.

policy against that, but Scott nixed the idea preemptively: "I thought it would really suck for our kids to lose both their dad and their uncle in one accident.") And while they insist there has never been any competition between them, their interplay suggests a gentle tweaking all the same. "Scott flew first," Mark says, "but I flew twice before he got his second flight. Then I flew my third before he did."

Over drinks at Boondoggles, an astronaut haunt in Houston, Scott describes a stubborn eye twitch he experienced during reentry after his previous mission, a 159-day stay aboard the space station that ended in 2011. It's something other long-duration astronauts have complained of too, but there is no explanation for it yet.

"What do you mean, your eyes twitched?" Mark asks.

"Yours didn't?" Scott responds.

"No."

"Your flights weren't long enough."

By shuttle standards, Mark's flights were actually pretty typical in terms of duration. His four trips ran about two weeks each, giving him a total of 54 days in space. Scott's first two flights were similar, but his 159-day stay put him at a running total of 180. With the just-completed mission, he vaults to 520.

A DAY IN ORBIT

As much of an adventure as Scott's mission was, neither Mark nor anyone else envied him every part of it. The ISS is spacious enough: from end to end, it measures 358 feet, a little larger than a football field. The 14 modules that make up the living and work space represent only a small fraction of that overall sprawl, but together they provide as much habitable space as the interior of a 747—or, as the astronauts prefer to think of it, as much as a six-bedroom house.

Still, stay inside any house for a year, even one in orbit, and you're going to fall into a routine. For all astronauts, a day aboard the station begins and ends in a private enclosure about the size of a phone booth that serves as sleep chamber and personal space, with enough room for a couple of laptop computers, a few belongings and a sleeping bag. Reveille, in the form of an alarm from a wristwatch or an iPad in each astronaut's enclosure, comes at about 6:30 a.m. GMT, but Scott admits that he often hit the snooze button. "I wouldn't wake up at the time it says on the schedule," he says. "I'd generally get 30 extra minutes of sleep."

When astronauts do crawl out of the sack, the day that unfolds usually follows a 30/40/30 work breakdown—30% of the time devoted to science experiments, 40% to physical exercise and monitoring the station's systems, and 30% to fixing hardware breakdowns—which is the way of things when your home requires 52 computers, 3.3 million lines of code, eight miles of wiring and 90 kilowatts of power coming from an acre of solar panels just to keep operating.

The daily schedule does allow for some downtime. Movies and books are stocked in the station, and NASA can send up nearly any TV program the astronauts request. The crew members are free to email family members whenever they want, call home when they've got a good downlink and surf the Internet, though the connection can be sluggish.

During the year in spaceflight, the time for distractions was especially tight, thanks to the battery of 10 medical and psychological tests that were on the agenda for both Scott and Kornienko in orbit as well as Mark on the ground. Flight surgeons ran—and are continuing to run—studies of cardiovascular efficiency, blood oxygen levels and blood volume. Bone density is monitored, as are cellular aging and fluid shifts in the body. Sonograms are taken of the eye and optic nerve to determine how those shifts affect vision.

The body's microbiome came in for scrutiny too. The bacteria that make their home in your gut are crucial to maintaining bodily function, but everyone's internal ecosystem is different, depending on diet and environment. The twins' microbiomes are regularly compared, via the unlovely business of analyzing body waste. "Giving urine and stool samples is an incredibly exciting thing to do," Mark says drily. But in the service of human spaceflight—even when that service is performed on the ground—it's worth the small indignity. "I miss every day I spent in space," Mark readily admits.

YOUR BRAIN ON SPACE TRAVEL

If the body can suffer from long-term spaceflight, the mind is hit even harder, and that causes NASA particular concern. Psychologists tracked Kornienko's and Scott's cognitive function, mood and stress level, partly via regular—and private—interviews. They were especially alert for what is known as the third-quarter effect, a slacking off of psychological performance that hits between the halfway and three-quarter points of any long confinement or tour of duty.

"Scott has flown a six-month mission, so we have data on him," said NASA psychologist Al Holland before the year aloft began. "But it's not a linear thing. Running a full marathon is different from running two half-marathons."

Here, the science must yield a bit to the wild card of human emotion, and even a veteran like Scott may have had trouble wrapping his mind around the scope of the mission he was about to undertake. His flight began on March 28, 2015, but he had to leave the U.S. on February 16, since he took off from the Russians' Baikonur launch complex. Before he left, Kauderer, his girlfriend, mused that since his birthday is February 21, he'd be 50 when he left the country and 52 when he came home. "I was like, 'Thanks for pointing that out,'" Scott says with a laugh.

It was easy to make jokes at T minus three months. Things got more difficult last spring, when the mission's 5,440 orbits got under way. It was then that the brother in space was especially fortunate to have the brother on the ground.

HOW ZERO-G AFFECTS THE HUMAN BODY

A look at some of the risks Scott Kelly and his fellow crew members faced on their yearlong mission—and possible ways to contain or reverse the damage

EYES
Vision can be damaged as fluids that are normally restrained by gravity migrate to the head, compressing the optic nerve and distorting the shape of the eyeball. Lower-body negative-pressure garments—think balloon pants—can help.

IMMUNE SYSTEM
The controlled environment of the space station can cause the immune system to slack off. Both Kelly brothers are getting flu vaccines to determine whether their reactions differ.

DIGESTION
Microorganisms populating the gut are essential for digestion and other functions. Diet and radiation damage this microbiome. Fruits and vegetables shipped to space on cargo runs may help restore balance.

MUSCLES
Muscles need the pull of gravity to stay strong and toned. Running on a treadmill—with bungee cords holding astronauts in place and simulating gravity—gives the legs a workout. Pulling against resistance can help exercise the arms.

MIND
A year of cosmic confinement is hard, especially months six through nine, researchers say, when fatigue sets in but the end is not yet in sight. Distractions like video chats and email with family can improve astronauts' moods and performance.

BLOOD
On Earth, the blood must flow uphill against gravity. In zero-G, the heart takes a while to adjust to the lower resistance. Blood pressure does eventually return to a healthy baseline; exercise can hurry that process along.

BONES
Bones that don't carry weight decalcify over time, so much so that newly arriving Russian cosmonauts have been discouraged from hugging those who have been aloft a long time, lest they break a rib. Exercise helps.

AGING
Caps on the ends of chromosomes called telomeres shorten throughout life, contributing to aging. In space, the telomere fuse burns faster. Scientists suspect numerous causes, including radiation and oxidative stress.

"This is a dangerous job," says Mark. "The public doesn't understand how dangerous. But Scott can talk to someone who's done this before."

During Scott's previous mission, it was Mark who had to lean on him—in January 2011, when Giffords was shot. NASA got the news up to Scott, and it was only later that the brothers could talk. For Mark, it wasn't quite the same. "The one person who could have given me the most support," he says, "was off the planet." During Scott's year in space, the support came from the ground up.

Mark has already retired from NASA but has not given up thoughts of returning to space one day. Scott has not decided whether he'll retire now that he's back on Earth. Either way, it's unlikely that the Kelly brothers, who once dreamed of building a rocket ship side by side, will ever fly in one together. But if humanity hopes to beat the biological limits that confine us to one small planet in a trackless universe, it will depend on the kind of science both brothers are making possible. Only one Kelly name was on the year-in-space mission patch, but to those who appreciate the brothers' bond, it stood for both.

Watch our video series A Year in Space *at time.com/space. For information on viewing the full-length documentary, go to pbs.org/yearinspace*

▲ At the Sonny Carter Training Facility in Houston in February 2015, Scott Kelly works in the Neutral Buoyancy Laboratory. Neutral-buoyancy training simulates the weightlessness experienced by astronauts in spaceflight.

// LIFTOFF!

ON AN EMOTIONAL DAY, THE CREW SAYS GOODBYE AND LEAVES THE EARTH BEHIND. NEXT STOP: THE INTERNATIONAL SPACE STATION

◀ At 1:42 a.m. on March 28, 2015, Scott Kelly, Mikhail Kornienko and Gennady Padalka roared off the launchpad in Baikonur, Kazakhstan. Just 11 minutes later, they were in orbit.

YOU'D THINK YOU'D HAVE TROUBLE deciding how to spend your last day on Earth if you were about to leave it for a year. But the fact is, you'd have nothing to decide at all. Every bit of it would be planned for you—literally second by second—as it was for Gennady Padalka, Mikhail Kornienko and Scott Kelly in advance of their liftoff at 1:42:57 a.m. local time in Baikonur, Kazakhstan, where the Russian launch facilities are located.

The three men were instructed to nap until nine hours before launch, or precisely 4:42:57 p.m. They left their quarters exactly one hour later, at 5:52:57 p.m., settled into the space center ready rooms and began their preflight preparations at 6:52:57. And on the day ticked. For the families, all those hours were a much more ambling business—time they had to contrive to fill on their own. As Kelly was getting his final hours of mandated terrestrial sleep, his daughters, Samantha and Charlotte, 20 and 11 at the time; his partner, Amiko Kauderer; and his brother, Mark, visited Baikonur's outdoor market in a hunt for spices Kauderer and

the girls wanted to take home.

Mark, who arrived in Baikonur still wearing his characteristic mustache—the only thing that allows most people to distinguish him from Scott—had shaved it off this morning. "Do I look like my brother now?" he asked, and then added mischievously, "Maybe I am."

Kauderer, who works as a NASA public-affairs officer and has witnessed her share of launches as well as her share of spouses steeling themselves for the experience, carried herself with the same apparent calm. So did the girls, who have seen their father fly off to space several times before. As for what Scott himself was feeling, Mark was sure it was nothing terribly special. "He's been through this four times already," he said. "Actually, when you count the times you don't launch, it's six or seven."

On launch day, the routine pressed on regardless of what Scott might or might not have been feeling. At 7:52 p.m., the crew, clad in blue jumpsuits, left the ready rooms for the 100-yard walk to the buses that would

▼ In a ceremony days before launch, officials from Roscosmos, Russia's space agency, hand off the Soyuz spacecraft to the prime crew and the backup crew of the one-year mission.

▲ Kornienko, Kelly and Padalka (from top) prepare to step onto the gantry elevator that will carry them up to their Soyuz rocket.

take them to the suit-up building. A rousing Russian song played over loudspeakers, while crowds were kept behind rope lines, both to prevent a crush and to protect the astronauts who were still under medical quarantine. Once they were sealed inside their bus, however, the lines collapsed and the crowd surged forward. A child was lifted to touch the window. Padalka pressed both of his hands on the glass while a woman reached up and pressed hers opposite them. In Russia, cosmonauts are every bit the cultural phenomenon they were half a century ago.

No one outside of flight technicians saw the crew again for two hours, until they had been suited up and the families were brought in for a final goodbye—the crew on one side of a glass partition and the loved ones on the other, communicating via microphones. "*Poka, poka*"—Russian for "bye-bye"—Padalka's daughters called to him. Mark, who made two visits to the space station on his shuttle flights, was less

sentimental. "I left some old T-shirts up in the gym," he said to his brother. "Want to bring them down for me?"

"You look good without that mustache," Scott answered.

"Yeah, I'll probably grow it back on the flight home. I miss it already."

Scott's exchanges with Amiko, Charlotte and Samantha were less playful, and afterward, when Roscosmos officials declared the five minutes allotted for the visit over, Amiko gathered the girls in a hug. "We have to hold it together," she says. "That's our job."

Finally, family, media and space officials left the suit-up building and walked to the parking lot just outside. The crew emerged a few minutes later to a fusillade of camera flashes and walked to three designated spots painted on the asphalt. American, Russian and Kazakh flags fluttered behind them and Roscosmos officials stood before them, bidding them a final goodbye. Padalka, the commander, stood in the middle during the ceremony, and he occupied the middle seat in the spacecraft as well.

A Soyuz veteran, Padalka has joked that he could fly the craft with nothing but a pair of cabbages in the seats on either side of him. Maybe. But if he meant that in the months he was training for this flight, there was no sign of it on the night he left. The crew, who would depend on one another for their lives, boarded their bus, drove to the pad and climbed into their spacecraft. Two and a half hours later, at the designated second, their Soyuz rocket's 20 engines lit, and they left Kazakhstan—and the planet—behind.

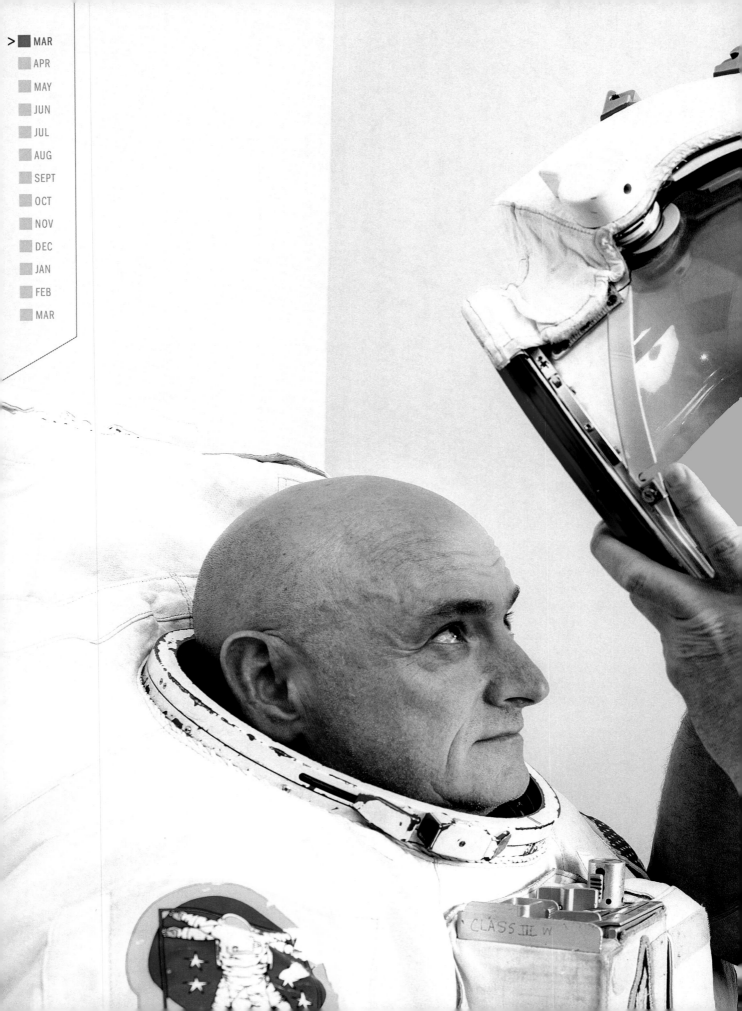

CLASS III W

// THE GREAT TWIN STUDY BEGINS

WHAT HAPPENS TO THE BODY IN SPACE?
BROTHERS MARK AND SCOTT KELLY GO UNDER
THE MICROSCOPE TO HELP FIND ANSWERS

◀ Scott and Mark Kelly are the only pair of siblings who have both traveled into space. Mark retired from the Navy and NASA in October 2011.

◀ The Kelly brothers, seen here at age 5, were born and grew up in, yes, Orange, N.J.

WHEN SERENDIPITY HANDS SCIEN-tists the perfect experiment, they don't hesitate to jump on it. That's surely the case with NASA's improbable study of Scott and Mark Kelly.

Zero gravity messes with the human body in all manner of ways, but it's not always easy to determine which problems are actually caused by the weightlessness and which ones would have happened anyway. The puzzle gets a lot easier if you just happen to have a second subject with exactly the same genes, the same lifestyle and the same level of fitness. Observe any differences in their health over the year, subtract the matching genetics, and what's left over on the other side of the equal sign is likely the work of weightlessness. Much of the research that was conducted while Scott was aloft involved collecting data on both twins; analyzing that data and following up on their health will take at least a year more.

One of the most important studies involves what are known as telomeres, the cuffs that pro-tect the tips of chromosomes in much the way that plastic aglets protect the tips of shoelaces. The longer we live, the shorter our telomeres get, and the unraveling of the chromosomes that results drives the infirmities that come with age.

"One of the things that comes up almost all the time in the interviews with Mark and Scott is this idea of the twin paradox," says Susan Bailey of Colorado State University, who is coordinating the telomere research. "Is the space twin going to come back younger than the Earth twin?" That kind of time dilation happens in movies like *Interstellar*, but only when someone is moving at close to light speed. The year Scott spent orbiting Earth at 17,150 miles per hour may indeed have slowed his body clock, but by barely a few milliseconds. His telomeres, however, more than made up for that, and he likely came home physically older than Mark.

"A whole variety of life stresses have been associated with accelerated telomere loss as we age," says Bailey. "You can imagine strapping yourself to a rocket and living in space for a year is a very stressful event."

Chromosomal samples from both Kelly twins were taken and banked before Scott left to provide a telomere baseline, and more samples were collected over the year.

Mark's were easy enough to get hold of, but Scott had to draw his own blood in space, spin it down and freeze it, then send it home aboard returning ships carrying cargo or astronauts. Both twins will be followed for two years after Scott's return to determine whether any space-related telomere loss slows and whether the brothers move closer to synchrony again.

The twins' blood samples will also be used to look for the state of their epigenomes, the chemical on-off switches that sit atop genomes and regulate which genes are expressed and which are silenced. Environment is a huge driver in epigenetic changes, especially in space, as cells adjust to the unfamiliar state of weight-lessness. "We can kind of build these molecular maps of what's happening in the different cells

. . . as they're challenged by this low-gravity condition," says geneticist Chris Mason of Weill Cornell Medical College in New York, who is leading this part of the work.

Also due for a good close look are Scott's and Mark's microbiomes. The number of cells that make up your body are outnumbered by the bacteria, viruses, yeasts and molds that live inside you and on your skin. It's only the fact that most of them are much smaller than human cells that prevents them from outweighing you. Still, if you could extract them all and hold them in your hand, they'd make a bolus of alien organisms weighing up to five pounds.

This is actually a good thing, since we need this microscopic ecosystem to keep our bodies—especially our digestive tract—running smoothly. Like so much else for Scott, that changed in space. "A significant part of what's present normally in the gastrointestinal tract doesn't actually colonize," says research professor Martha Vitaterna of Northwestern University, the co-investigator on the microbiome work.

THE YEAR SCOTT SPENT ORBITING EARTH MAY HAVE SLOWED HIS BODY CLOCK, BUT HE LIKELY RETURNS HOME PHYSICALLY OLDER THAN HIS BROTHER.

◀ The Kelly brothers match again, this time after a baseball game in 1971.

◄ Scott and Mark Kelly, born on Feb. 21, 1964, have each completed four space missions.

▲ At the Johnson Space Center on August 10, flight controllers at ISS Mission Control keep an eye on a space walk (left) and the crew as it samples salad grown in space (right).

"These are things that are constantly being reintroduced with fresh fruits and vegetables, and that's missing from Scott's diet."

Genes can also make a difference to the microbiome, since any individual's genetic makeup may determine which microorganisms thrive in the gut and which don't. Scott's and Mark's microbiomes were compared throughout the year, principally through stool samples—which ensured some unglamorous if scientifically essential shipments coming down from space.

Other studies involved the way body fluids shifted in zero-G and the issues it caused, from pressure on the eyeballs to damage to the cardiovascular system.

Some of these changes are being tracked by blood studies, which look for proteins that regulate water excretion. Ultrasound scans can also look for vascular damage. Before leaving Earth, Scott had a few small dots tattooed on his upper body to indicate the exact points at which he had to position the ultrasound probe—easier than taking precise measurements to find the proper spots every time he was due for a scan.

Multiple other studies are being conducted on the twins as well, looking at their immune systems, sleep cycles, psychological states and more. For years, space planners have been talking a good game about going to Mars one day. We know the hardware can survive the journey; what we don't know is if the human cargo can. Before long—thanks to the Kellys—we'll be a lot smarter.

// AT HOME
ABOVE THE WORLD

SCOTT KELLY AND MIKHAIL KORNIENKO SETTLE INTO A ROUTINE
OF MAINTENANCE, LAB WORK AND MOVIE NIGHTS

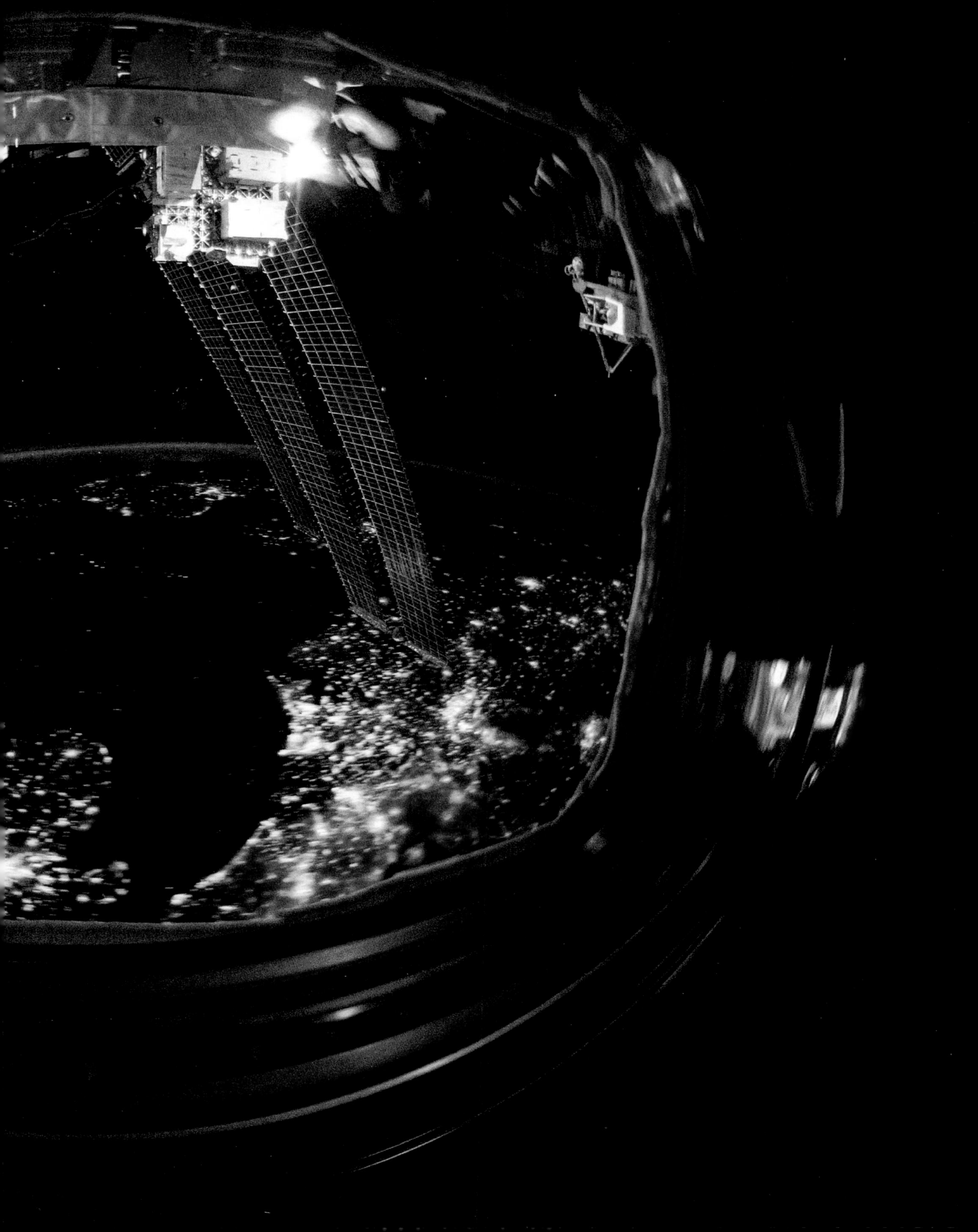

◀ A view of the ISS's solar array from inside the station

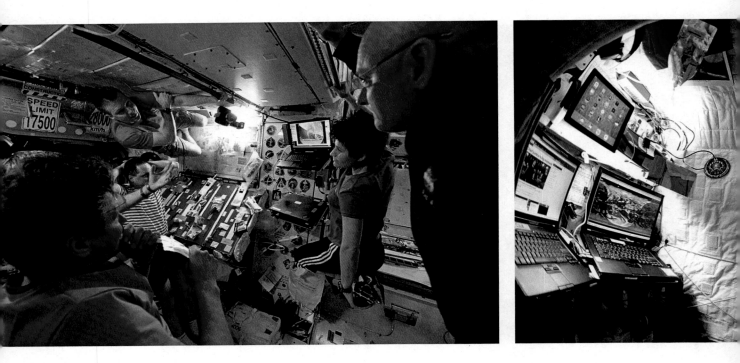

A YEAR IN SPACE IS MARKED IN PART by the holidays that pass while you're away. Christmas? Sorry, out of town. Easter? Ditto. Thanksgiving, New Year's Eve, Halloween? Catch you next year.

It's fitting, then, that the first holiday astronaut Scott Kelly spent in the first month of his stay aboard the International Space Station was Cosmonautics Day. Never heard of it? You would have if you were Russian.

Cosmonautics Day celebrates April 12, 1961, when Yuri Gagarin lifted off from the same launchpad from which Kelly's mission began, becoming the first human being in space. Kelly and his five crewmates got the morning off on that special day, taking the opportunity to enjoy the relative comforts of a spacecraft with more habitable space than a six-bedroom home. But in the afternoon it was back to work—following a moment-by-moment schedule that was scripted on the ground, that was adhered to in space and that, while often grueling, is the best way for astronauts and cosmonauts who have signed on for a long hitch to focus on their work and keep the time from crawling.

Kelly's first month was, in some ways, typical of the 11 that followed. There was the arrival of a SpaceX cargo ship, a vessel carrying 4,300 pounds of equipment and supplies, including a subzero freezer that can preserve experiments

at –112°F, that needed to be unloaded; new gear to aid studies of the effects of microgravity on mice; and a sample of so-called synthetic muscle, a strong but pliant material modeled after human muscle, to be used for robotic limbs and joints. Also tucked into the load was a less practical but infinitely more anticipated item: a zero-gravity espresso machine, dubbed the ISSpresso.

There are 250 experiments that must be tended to at any one time aboard the ISS, but the most important of them in the past year were Kelly and cosmonaut Mikhail Kornienko themselves. In their first month in space, the two long-termers submitted to a whole range of preliminary experiments that tracked their

KELLY HAD LEISURE ACTIVITIES TO LOOK FORWARD TO: WEB SURFING, AND REGULAR VIDEO CHATS, PHONE CALLS AND EMAILS WITH FAMILY.

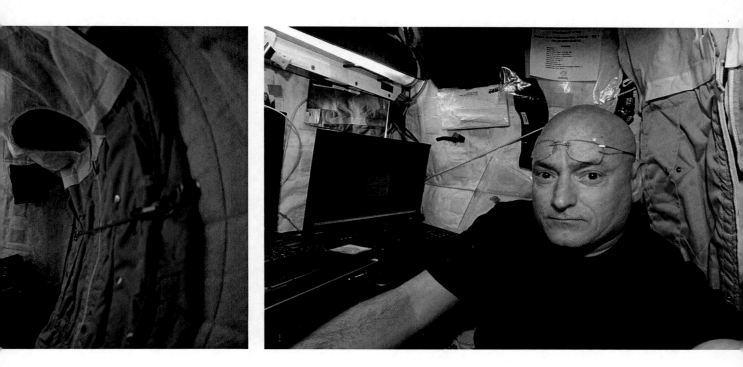

▲ The galley (left) includes an angled surface where food packets can be attached with Velcro. Kelly's sleeping quarters (center and right) afford him a measure of privacy. The green sleeping bag can hang upright because there are no "up" and "down" in space.

health throughout their stay. Space physicians already know the basic answer; it's not a good one. But the hope is that Kelly and Kornienko will help provide ways to mitigate damage.

Biomedical studies in the first month included seeing how the upward shift of fluids in the body affected the eyes; sampling saliva and sweat to test for bacterial levels and chemical balance; leg scans to determine blood flow; studies of blood pressure, which can fluctuate wildly when the heart no longer has to pump against gravity; analyses of throat and skin samples; and bone-density tests.

The 11 months that followed were not all a Groundhog Day repetition of the first. Kelly was scheduled for two space walks, the first of his four-mission career, to conduct basic maintenance work and help oversee a complex reconfiguration of the station, with modules and docking ports repositioned to accommodate commercial crew vehicles built by Boeing and SpaceX, which are supposed to begin arriving in 2017. He spent long hours preparing for the walks, training in NASA's Neutral Buoyancy

Lab, a 6.2-million-gallon pool in Houston with a full-size mock-up of the station resting on its bottom. Weights in the buoyant spacesuit ensure that an astronaut neither floats up nor sinks, mirroring the drifting-in-place experience of walking in space.

But work—even thrilling work like a space walk—could not be all there was to sustain an astronaut spending a year aloft, and so Kelly also had free time and leisure activities to look forward to: movie nights, Web surfing, and regular video chats, phone calls and emails with family. The periodic arrivals of cargo ships provided such luxuries as fresh fruits and vegetables—which don't last long in space, but they don't have to, because six-person crews missing the comforts of home scarf them down quickly.

The clubhouse turn of Kelly and Kornienko's one-year mission occurred in December 2015, the 50th anniversary of what was once America's longest stay in space: the two-week flight of Gemini 7, which astronauts Frank Borman and Jim Lovell passed in the equivalent of two coach airline seats, with the ceiling just three inches over their heads. The ISS is a manor house compared with the Gemini. But the astronauts are still astronauts, human beings in a very strange place experiencing very strange things—in some cases for a very long time.

// LANDSCAPE MODE

DURING HIS YEAR IN SPACE, SCOTT KELLY KEPT AN EXTRAORDINARY VISUAL DIARY, USING HIS CAMERAS TO CAPTURE THE WORLD INSIDE AND OUTSIDE THE ISS. HIS IMAGES, POSTED ON SOCIAL MEDIA, REVEALED THE GLOBE'S GEOGRAPHY IN JOYOUS, GHOSTLY AND UNEXPECTED WAYS

◄ Tajikistan, bordering China and Afghanistan, is famous for its stunning mountain ranges. Scott Kelly posted this photo in April 2015.

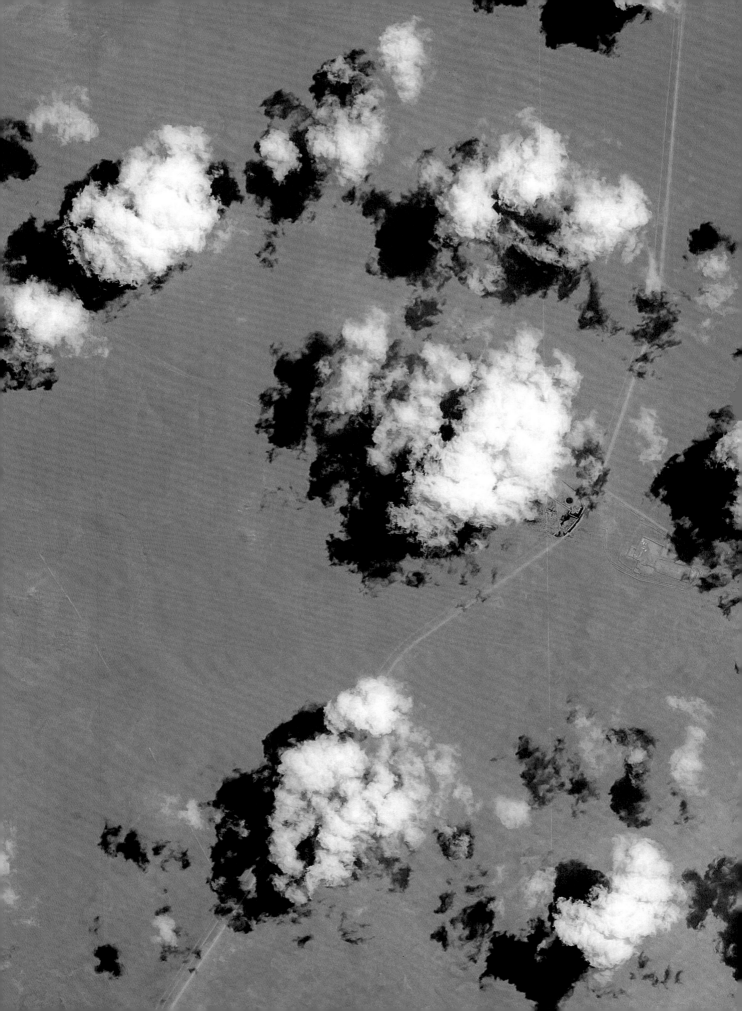

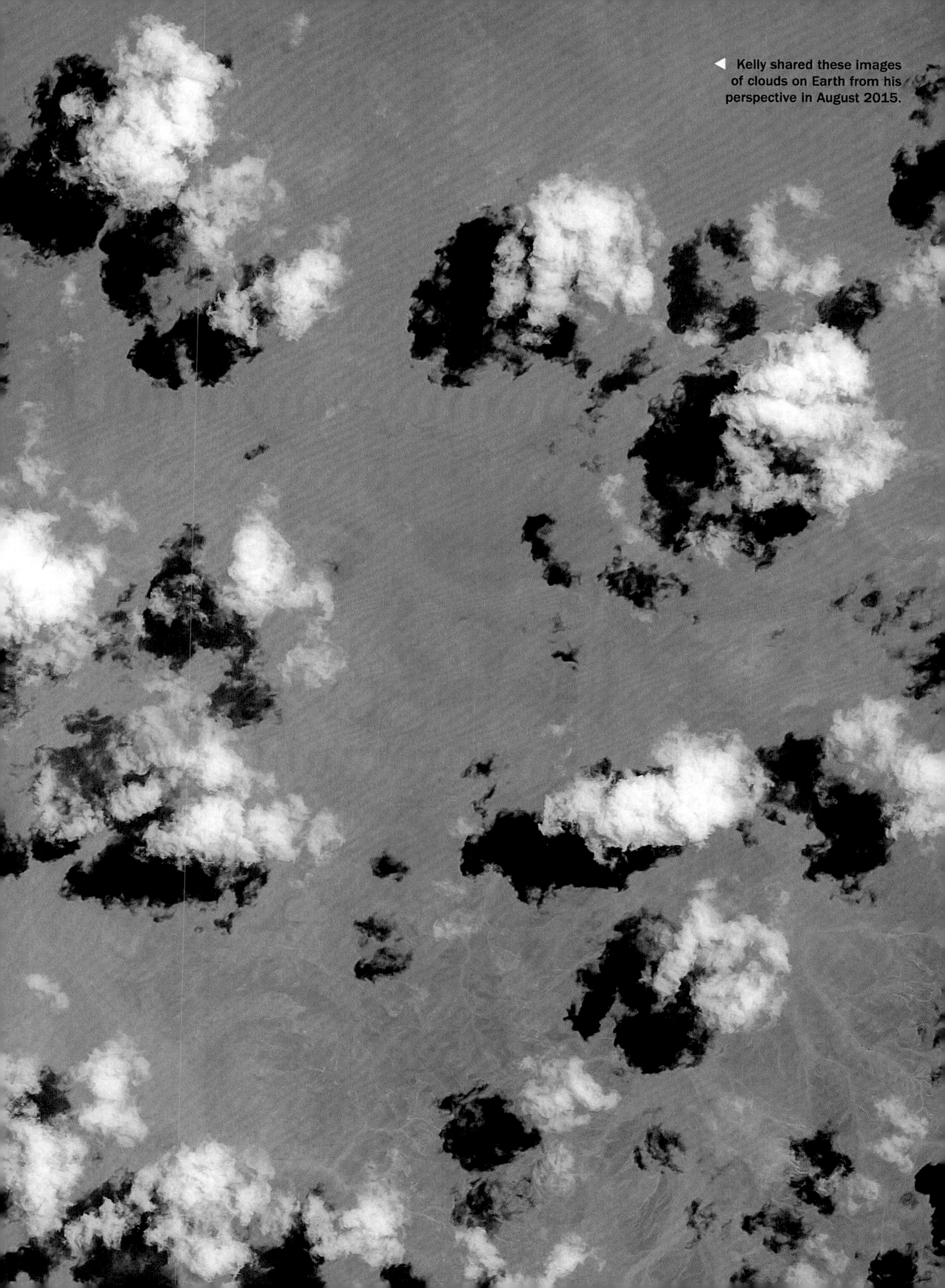

Kelly shared these images of clouds on Earth from his perspective in August 2015.

▶ Kelly took this photo while flying over Madagascar in April 2015.

MAR
APR
MAY
JUN
JUL
AUG
SEPT
OCT
NOV
DEC
JAN
FEB
MAR

// GETTING THE WORK DONE

THE ASTRONAUTS TACKLE MUST-DO TASKS WHILE MOVING 17,150 MILES PER HOUR, 250 MILES HIGH IN THE SKY

Scott Kelly and Terry Virts conduct eye exams inside the Destiny Laboratory. Astronauts suffer numerous vision problems in zero gravity, so testing becomes crucial in preparing for longer space travel.

HOW DID YOUR PRE-TREATED URINE transfer rate work out this week? I'm sorry? You had no pre-treated urine transfer rate to worry about? Oh, then you must not be aboard the International Space Station.

It was a busy first three months in space for Scott Kelly and Misha Kornienko, as well as for the rest of the crew aboard the ISS, which pretty much describes all of their days. If there's one point astronauts mention about their time aloft, it's the challenge of the schedule: the long, every-minute-accounted-for checklist of tasks that have to be completed every single day. Some of them are the glamour stuff of space

travel—space walks, formation flying with arriving vehicles, TV broadcasts to the folks back home. Some are a good deal more mundane, such as troubleshooting the stubbornly low flow rate in a system that is supposed to filter and recycle urine into ordinary drinking water.

Mission planners are not shy about revealing just how hard they make the astronauts work, as a glimpse at NASA's ISS blog reveals. On May 22, for example, the crew woke up to a list of 65 must-do items; three days later it was 67; the following day was a light day in comparison, with a scant 55. A lot of what was done on those days was very big stuff. On May 26, Kelly and crewmate Terry Virts oversaw the transfer of

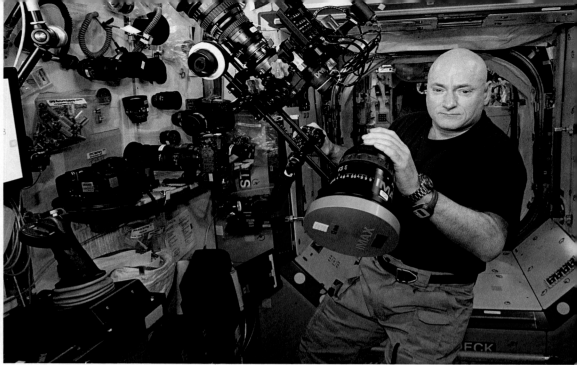

◀ What looks like a surgical tray with implements (left) is actually a kitchen counter where meals are prepared from packaged foods. The table is inclined at a 45-degree angle to save space. ▲ Above, Kelly works with some of the many cameras and lenses aboard the ISS. ▶ At right, Kelly and Terry Virts work on a Carbon Dioxide Removal Assembly to keep the cabin air safe for the crew.

the Permanent Multipurpose Module (PMM) from one berthing site on the station to another, which is both much more important and more difficult than it sounds. For one thing, the module weighs 11 tons. And like most station modules, it's roughly the size of a school bus.

Relocating it meant three control centers had to work in tandem: Mission Control in Houston; the Mobile Servicing Systems Operations Center in Quebec, which oversees the work of the station's robotic arm; and the station itself, with Kelly and Virts in charge. The goal was to decouple the PMM from the Unity module and move it to the nearby Tranquility module—by remote control, while moving 17,150 miles per hour, at an altitude of 250 miles.

But it was worth the effort. By 2017, two new commercial crew vehicles built by Boeing and SpaceX will begin flying to the station, freeing the U.S. from its reliance on Russia's Soyuz. That called for reconfiguring the station to open up the best docking ports to receive crew— and that meant the PMM had to find somewhere else to live.

A lot of the other work continued the extensive biomedical tests on Kelly, Kornienko and the other astronauts to study the human body's fitness for long-term spaceflight. For example, Kelly and Kornienko went through their paces with fine-motor-skill tests, tapping at touch-

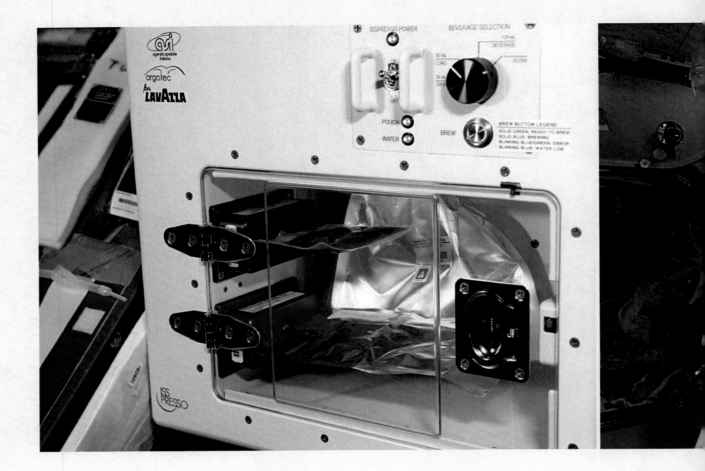

SIPPING COFFEE IN SPACE COULD HELP SAVE LIVES ON EARTH

The so-called space cups can reveal much about fluid physics

ASTRONAUTS ABOARD THE International Space Station can now enjoy a much-needed cup of joe with their own espresso machine and a set of six microgravity coffee cups—which are really more like jugs, but never mind. Whatever you call them, the containers do more than just offer astronauts a little earthly luxury; they may also provide scientists with data on how complex fluids move in zero gravity. Before the invention of the space cup, astronauts had to drink by sucking liquid out of a bag, a technique that's been used since the earliest days of the space age. The new cups have a sharp inner corner that allows the liquid to be pushed along the inside of the interior wall—a process called capillary action—toward the drinker's lips. By experimenting with capillary physics in small containers like these, scientists believe they can build better advanced fluid systems for use in space. This could improve delivery of coolants and fuel and improve the function of air conditioners, toilets and recycling systems. The same data—and similar physics—could also be put to work on Earth in devices like portable diagnostic devices used to test blood for infectious diseases in remote areas of the world. It may be only NASA that would require two investigators, one developer and a project name to invent a coffee cup, but it also may be only NASA that could find so valuable an earthly use for it.

AN EXPERIMENT WITH ULTRASOUND EQUIPMENT TRACKS HOW SHIFTING BODY FLUID AFFECTS THE SHAPE OF THE EYEBALL.

screens to measure reaction time and dexterity; the results will reflect how those functions changed over the course of their stay.

Kelly and cosmonaut Gennady Padalka worked with ultrasound equipment to help study how fluid shifting from the lower body to the head affects the shape of the eyeball and the condition of the optic nerve. In addition, Kelly underwent similar testing while wearing a CHIBIS lower-body negative-pressure suit, which pulls fluid back down from the head and reduces the pressure that causes the damage. Yes, a more colloquial description of a CHIBIS lower-body negative-pressure suit is "rubber vacuum pants"—but if your vision depended on them, you'd be happy to put them on too.

Other work on the station involved echocardiograms, with crew members serving sometimes as crew medical officers (CMOs) and sometimes as patients, as they performed scans on one another; experiments on convection, fluid physics and the effects of the space environment on various materials subjected to long-term exposure outside the station; and maintenance work on extravehicular activity (EVA) suits in preparation for future space walks.

None of the work was easy, some of it was monotonous, and all of it just kept coming. Before leaving for space, Kelly reflected on the previous time he was aboard the ISS, which was a comparatively brief six months. The biggest adjustment, he said, was realizing that he could return home, sit on the couch and do nothing at all if he chose. Now, after a full year in space, that's probably an adjustment he doesn't mind a bit.

▲ The ISSpresso, shown at top left, allows the crew to brew coffee, tea and other hot beverages. Italian astronaut Samantha Cristoforetti sampled a batch of java and tweeted her verdict: "Not too bad." Above: Scott Kelly posted this image of a droplet of orbital espresso sitting at the end of a drinking straw.

APR
> MAY
JUN
JUL
AUG
SEPT
OCT
NOV
DEC
JAN
FEB
MAR

// LABS AND LEISURE TIME

THE CREW STUDIES SKIN AND CELEBRATES STAR WARS DAY

*T*HINK YOU'RE COOL BECAUSE YOU hosted a *Star Wars*–watching party on May 4, a date recognized as Star Wars Day? (May the fourth be with you and all that.) Well, you're not as cool as you think. Watching *Star Wars* when you're 250 miles above Earth, orbiting the planet aboard the International Space Station—now that's cool. That's how Scott Kelly and Mikhail Kornienko, along with the other members of the ISS crew, spent a few hours of downtime that day.

The year in space was not without earthly grace notes. There were tacos—or the closest approximation of them when you're using rehydrated food—the next day, in honor of Cinco de Mayo. And there was espresso, thanks to the newly delivered machine, dubbed the ISSpresso, which Italian astronaut Samantha Cristoforetti set up. "Coffee: the finest organic suspension ever devised," she tweeted. "Fresh espresso in the new Zero-G cup! To boldly brew . . ."

But there was more than good food and good films happening on the station. Take the mouse studies, which are routinely conducted in orbit but took on special importance in the context of the biomedical research at the heart of Kelly's

and Kornienko's marathon stay. Zero-G can be as hard for mice to manage as it is for human beings, and they spend a lot of time in their enclosures just trying to get oriented. Conducting experiments on them is hard too, since you don't want to open a habitat just anywhere and have an escapee drift free and get lost.

So mouse enclosures must be anchored on an experimental rack; lights, fans and power connectors have to be engaged; food bars must be provided. The research focuses on the animals' skeletal, muscular, immune and cardio-vascular systems. But unlike human subjects, mice can be, well, sacrificed and dissected to provide more detailed looks at what's going on.

Cristoforetti spent time working on the straightforwardly if unartfully named Skin-B study, which involves analyzing cells and tissue

> ### ZERO-G CAN BE AS HARD FOR MICE AS IT IS FOR HUMANS, AND THEY SPEND A LOT OF TIME JUST GETTING ORIENTED.

◀ Scott Kelly prepared an egg, sausage and tortilla taco to celebrate Cinco de Mayo while watching the Houston news (opposite, left). Terry Virts and Kelly are seen (opposite, right) hard at work during a cargo transfer. ▲ Above, Kelly, a *Star Wars* fan, worked with experimental spherical satellites in a 2010 expedition. He retweeted the photo in December 2015 with the caption "Wait these are the droids we're looking for."

samples to determine why human skin ages so much faster in zero-G than it does on Earth. That should not happen, since much of what causes the ordinary stretching and breakdown of skin is gravity, which is not a factor in space. But what *should* happen and what *does* happen are often two different things in science, and Cristoforetti was put to work learning why.

Skin is the body's largest organ, and it pays to know why it suffers so much in zero-G. Both in space and on the ground, what's learned from Skin-B could also provide insight into the functioning—and malfunctioning—of other organs, especially the ones lined with epithelial cells, the type of cells that make up the skin.

In May 2015, American astronaut Terry Virts, the commander of the ISS, busied himself in the Japan-built Kibo module, getting ready for the next round of Robot Refueling Mission-2 (RRM-2) exercises. RRM-2 explores ways to repair, upgrade and refuel satellites in orbit, using robots instead of astronauts to do the dangerous work. Satellite servicing was one of the big selling points of the space shuttle, and while the on-

call repair-visit routine never became routine, some of the most impressive of the shuttles' missions were the maintenance trips astronauts made to the Hubble Space Telescope.

Least important to the station's science objectives, perhaps, but most important to its crew were preparations Kelly and Virts made to replace the filters that scrub carbon dioxide from the ISS atmosphere. Remember the scene in the film *Apollo 13* in which the astronauts had to figure out how to make a replacement filter from cardboard, plastic bags and duct tape or they would suffocate on their own exhalations? The station crew doesn't want to have to do that—so Kelly and Virts had to get things right.

That's the rub about any given week on the ISS: maintenance jobs can be routine—but only until they're critical. The science can seem arcane—but only until it revolutionizes our knowledge of human biology. Kelly and Kornienko had less than a year's worth of time to do their otherworldly work, and the other crew members have up to six months each. The rest of us have forever to use the knowledge they bring home.

MAR
APR
> MAY
JUN
JUL
AUG
SEPT
OCT
NOV
DEC
JAN
FEB
MAR

Fluids & Combustion Facility (FCF)

// THE
SPACE
SHOT

*HOW A VACCINE EXPERIMENT ABOARD
THE ISS MAY HELP US BACK ON EARTH*

▲ Scott Kelly self-administers a flu vaccine to help study how the immune system behaves in zero-G. He will get another now that he's home.

YOU'D THINK IT WOULD BE HARD TO get sick in space. There is no part of your body the medics wouldn't have turned inside out looking for problems; you'd have been placed in medical quarantine for days before launch; and once you did take off, well, goodbye Earth, with all its colds and flus and walking pneumonias. The bugs are down there and you're up here.

But that's not the way things work. Bacteria and viruses adore the environment of a spacecraft: it's warm, it's sealed, it's climate-controlled, and the air circulates and circulates. Best of all, it's full of people who have nowhere to go and no way to avoid sharing stray germs.

That's especially true aboard the ISS, where crews rotate in and out and can stay for many months at a time, and where residents' immune systems—flummoxed by long-term exposure to zero-G—are unable to function as they should. But NASA is taking an important step toward solving these problems, with the imaginative study of Scott Kelly and his twin brother Mark. The cutting-edge, space-age tool that will be central to the work? The ordinary flu vaccine.

The Kelly brothers' immune systems had already been studied in the run-up to Scott's launch in March 2015, and both men were certified fit. But they should have slowly diverged over the course of the year. In space, some of the immune system's billions of cells begin to change in shape and function, especially the critical T-cells—and none of it is for the better.

"There is suppression of T-cell activation pathways," says Emmanuel Mignot, an immune-system specialist and one of the year-in-space mission's medical investigators. "They are the generals that coordinate the entire immune response."

Making things worse, while the ISS is hardly germ-free, it's a lot more antiseptic than Earth is, and that means the body can get forgetful, unlearning some of the immunities it has acquired over the years. "The immune system needs to be challenged," says Mignot. If it isn't, it grows slack—and its owner gets sick.

The experiment that will help study all of this began a few months before Scott even left Earth, when both brothers received a common trivalent flu vaccine—one that is formulated to protect against three strains of the virus. Blood was drawn from both men seven days later, which is typically the point at which the immune response peaks and the greatest number of cells that have been mustered to respond to the vaccine are present.

In November 2015, as flu season was getting under way on Earth, both brothers were vaccinated again—Scott in space and Mark on the ground—and more blood was drawn. Scott's sample was frozen and returned to Earth aboard one of the unmanned cargo runs flown by the SpaceX Dragon. Now that Scott is back on the ground, there will be a final round of vaccines and blood draws in November 2016.

In all of the samples, Mignot is scrutinizing the brothers' twin immune responses in ways that haven't been possible before. "We'll be using a new technique that recognizes just

SICK IN SPACE

The most famous incident of illness aboard a mission involved Apollo 7 in 1968, when commander Wally Schirra got sick and infected his crewmates. But a handful of other flights have been plagued as well:

APOLLO 8
1968
Frank Borman had what may have been a bad reaction to a sleeping pill. He discovered that bodily fluids are not easy to clean in space.

APOLLO 13
1970
This flight had a couple of health alarms— Ken Mattingly left the crew before the flight after being exposed to measles, and then Fred Haise endured a urinary-tract infection.

EUROPEAN SPACE AGENCY STS-122
2008
German astronaut Hans Schlegel may have had a bout of space sickness during a shuttle mission. He had to opt out of a scheduled space walk.

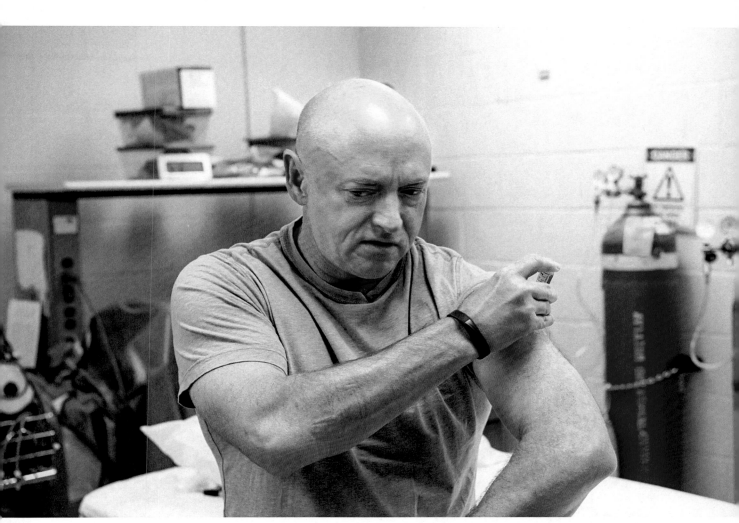

▲ Mark Kelly is following the same vaccine regimen as his brother so that their immune systems can be compared. On Earth he could let a doctor do the job, but in solidarity with Scott, he does it himself.

pieces of the virus," he says. "It's quite sophisticated; we'll have ideas of both the strength and qualitative nature of the immune response."

Mignot and the other NASA researchers will be looking not just at how Scott's immune system was changed by his time in space but also how well it recovers once he's back on Earth. The results could have implications that go beyond the ISS, affecting people with compromised immune systems due to chemotherapy, congenital conditions or diseases like HIV/AIDS.

Mignot also hopes that vaccine research aboard the ISS will pay one other dividend: reminding parents and others that vaccines are safe and effective and that scare stories about the shots causing disease are just that—scare stories.

"Vaccines are incredibly safe," he says. "Don't be crazy and let diseases like measles and polio get started again." Communicating a basic health message is not why the vaccine study was designed for the ISS, but it is one more reminder of the program's guiding idea: it is research conducted "off the Earth, for the Earth."

THE ISS IS A LOT MORE ANTISEPTIC THAN EARTH, AND THAT MEANS THE BODY CAN GROW FORGETFUL, UNLEARNING SOME IMMUNITIES IT HAS ACQUIRED.

FIVE WAYS MEDICINE IN SPACE IS COMPLETELY DIFFERENT FROM ON EARTH

Things change in zero-G

YOU MAY OR MAY NOT WANT TO GO TO SPACE, but here's something certain: you definitely don't want to get sick there. Ask the crew of Apollo 7, the 1968 mission in which the commander contracted a cold and spread it to the other two astronauts and all three of them spent the entire mission trapped inside a cramped spacecraft, sneezing, hacking and griping at the ground.

And that was just 11 days in Earth orbit. What about a year aboard the International Space Station? What about a two-and-a-half-year mission to Mars? And what about something a wee bit more serious than a cold, like appendicitis or a heart attack or a severe injury? NASA planners got a glimpse of what this could be like in 1999, when Jerri Nielsen, a physician working at a South Pole research station, diagnosed herself with breast cancer. It was impossible for anyone to rescue her during the Antarctic winter, and the best the U.S. Air Force could do was to drop chemotherapy drugs to her by parachute and wait for conditions to improve. In space, things would be far more dire.

These are some of the scenarios that were on the mind of rookie astronaut Kjell Lindgren, who spent nearly five months aboard the ISS over the past year. Lindgren is not just a well-trained astronaut but a specialist in aerospace and emergency medicine—just the kind of expert who will increasingly be needed as the human presence in space becomes permanent.

"If we want to go to Mars someday," Lindgren said in a conversation with TIME, "if we want to get further and deeper into the solar system, we need to start thinking about these things—thinking about the capabilities we need to do an appendectomy or take out a gall bladder."

There were no gall bladder or appendix takings while Lindgren was aloft. During the stint, he and the ISS flight doctors back on Earth took only space-medicine baby steps, learning the basics about the radical differences between medical care on Earth and medical care off it. Here are a few of the most vexing problems they have addressed:

1 WHERE IS THAT KIDNEY AGAIN?

On Earth, a person's organs settle into predictable positions. A doctor palpating a liver or thumping a patient's chest knows exactly where things ought to be. In zero-G, not so much. "The organs may be displaced a little bit," says Lindgren. "They tend to shift up a little more. The heart may have a little bit of a different orientation, which may be reflected on an EKG."

2 TREATING EYE ISSUES

Astronauts who have been in space for long-term stays often find that their vision grows worse, and it doesn't always bounce back completely when they return to Earth. (The problem is caused by fluid shifting upward from the lower body into the head.) Eye infections and irritation are more common too, for decidedly ick-inducing reasons. "Dust doesn't settle in the vehicle like it does on Earth," says Lindgren. "So things are liberated; little pieces of metal from equipment or maybe dead skin just float around and cause eye irritation."

3 MIND THE FEET

The calluses that build up on the heel and the ball of a person's foot after a lifetime of walking around serve a purpose, which is to cushion the foot against the shock of walking. Since walking is one thing weightless astronauts are not doing in space, they don't need the calluses. But ISS crew members need to beware when they remove their socks—the calluses may slough off, so the wrong move at the wrong time could leave unsightly bits of astronaut foot floating around the cabin.

▲ Astronauts Kjell Lindgren (left) and Scott Kelly sample red lettuce grown aboard the space station. An earlier crew grew a similar crop and shipped the plants home first to test for safety and palatability.

plants in a sickly glow, making them altogether unappetizing until they're harvested. So green lights are added to "enhance the human visual perception of the plants," said Wheeler.

Nothing, however, goes onto the astronauts' menu—or into their bodies—without being rigorously tested first. In May 2014 an earlier crew germinated the first plant pillows, grew them for 33 days, then plucked and froze them and shipped them home on a returning spacecraft in October. Scientists on the ground certified them fit to eat, so Kelly germinated a new

batch on July 7 ,and he and crewmates Kjell Lindgren and Kimiya Yui sampled them on August 10. They pronounced them fine.

There is one more reason to keep a garden running in space—and that explains why there are other pillows containing zinnia seeds aboard. The flowers are edible, yes, but they're also beautiful and colorful and fun to tend. Gardening is a very earthly grace note and has long been thought of as a relaxing and satisfying way for astronauts to keep themselves busy on long-duration missions that can quickly settle into repetitiveness and drudgery.

"The farther and longer humans go away from Earth, the greater the need to be able to grow plants for food, atmosphere recycling and psychological benefits," said Gioia Massa, Veggie's payload scientist. "I think that plant systems will become important components of any long-duration exploration scenario."

That's a whole lot of expectation riding on what is, today, just a few leaves of red romaine. But early homesteaders got their start with just small garden plots too. There's no reason their 21st-century heirs can't do the same.

"THE FARTHER AND LONGER HUMANS GO AWAY FROM EARTH, THE GREATER THE NEED TO BE ABLE TO GROW PLANTS FOR FOOD."

—SCIENTIST GIOIA MASSA

// DOCKING MANEUVERS

TO MAKE THINGS EASIER FOR AN ARRIVING SPACECRAFT, THE CREW MOVES ITS SOYUZ TO A NEW PORT

▲ Cosmonaut Yuri Malenchenko docks the Soyuz TMA-19M spacecraft to the ISS's Rassvet module in December 2015. The initial automatic mooring plan didn't work out, so Malenchenko had to guide the Soyuz manually.

*O*NE OF THE TRICKIEST QUESTIONS for a Soyuz spacecraft approaching the International Space Station is where to park. The ISS may be larger than a football field, but it's got only so many ways to get inside it, and with crewed spacecraft and uncrewed cargo ships regularly shuttling up and down, docking ports—or at least the right docking port—can be at a premium.

In the pre-dawn hours of September 28, Space Station astronaut Scott Kelly, along with cosmonauts Mikhail Kornienko and Gennady Padalka, were required to do a bit of delicate flying to sort out just that kind of problem.

Their Soyuz spacecraft was docked at the station's Poisk module—a 16-foot Russian node that was added to the ISS in 2009 as a science lab, observation point and egress compartment for astronauts embarking on space walks. The Soyuz had been there since Kelly arrived in March 2015, and that was a concern.

For five months, the ship had been hanging off the station in the alternating searing heat and deep freeze of orbital space. The conditions can take a toll on vessels' hardware, and since the crews rely on them as their way back to Earth, NASA and the Russian space agency, Roscosmos, had instituted a rule: 180 days is the maximum amount of time a Soyuz can remain aloft before detaching and returning to Earth. But Kelly and Kornienko were set to stay twice as long as that—which complicated their ride home.

Their Soyuz was not the only one on hand. There was another one for the other three crew members who were aboard. (Another NASA-Roscosmos rule: there must always be enough seats for everyone to be able to bail out immediately in the event of an emergency.) And a third ship, carrying three more crew members for a change of personnel, was set to arrive. Since the Poisk module faces Earth, it is the easiest target for approaching spacecraft. But freeing the dock required a little juggling. Mission rules, to say nothing of basic physics, made the job a delicate one.

At 3:09 a.m. EDT, the complete Padalka-Kornienko-Kelly team climbed fully suited into their Soyuz. Technically, it did not take all three men to do the job. Padalka, who is one of the most experienced Soyuz pilots extant,

FIVE-PLUS MONTHS HANGING OFF THE ISS IN ALTERNATING SEARING HEAT AND DEEP FREEZE CAN TAKE A TOLL ON A SPACECRAFT'S HARDWARE.

could probably have handled matters on his own. But in the event of a Soyuz emergency requiring an immediate reentry, all three men were required to be aboard—lest a solitary pilot return home, leaving five people aboard the ISS and only three seats on the remaining Soyuz.

The crew then undocked from the Poisk and re-docked to the nearby Zvezda module, or service module—a straight distance of only a few dozen yards. These kinds of orbital maneuvers require care, with both the station and the Soyuz orbiting the Earth at 17,150 miles per hour but moving just a few feet or inches at a time relative to each other.

"They'll undock, then back out 200 meters or so," said NASA TV commentator and overall space-station authority Rob Navias, before the maneuver. "Then they'll fly around to the back end of the service module, do a lateral translation, fly retrograde, then move in for a docking at the aft end of the module." If that sounds like an awfully complicated way to say, essentially, that they would back up, turn around and pull in at another door, it's less technobabble than it is a reflection of the complexity of even the most straightforward maneuvers in space.

Two of the newly arriving crew members were only short-timers, staying on the station for just 10 days. They then flew home with Padalka in the older ship, leaving the fresh one for Kelly, Kornienko and another crew member six months later: their trip home on March 2, 2016.

The ISS may be the most complicated job site on—or off—the planet, but it's one that could proudly display a sign reading 15 YEARS WITHOUT AN ACCIDENT. Playing by all the workplace safety rules will help keep that record going.

▲ Above: the Soyuz TMA-15M is docked at the ISS in May 2015. The spacecraft later carried Terry Virts, Samantha Cristoforetti and Russian cosmonaut Anton Shkaplerov back to Earth.
◄ Left: Scott Kelly snapped this photo of the Soyuz TMA-17M bringing crew members Kjell Lindgren, Oleg Kononenko and Kimiya Yui home in December 2015.

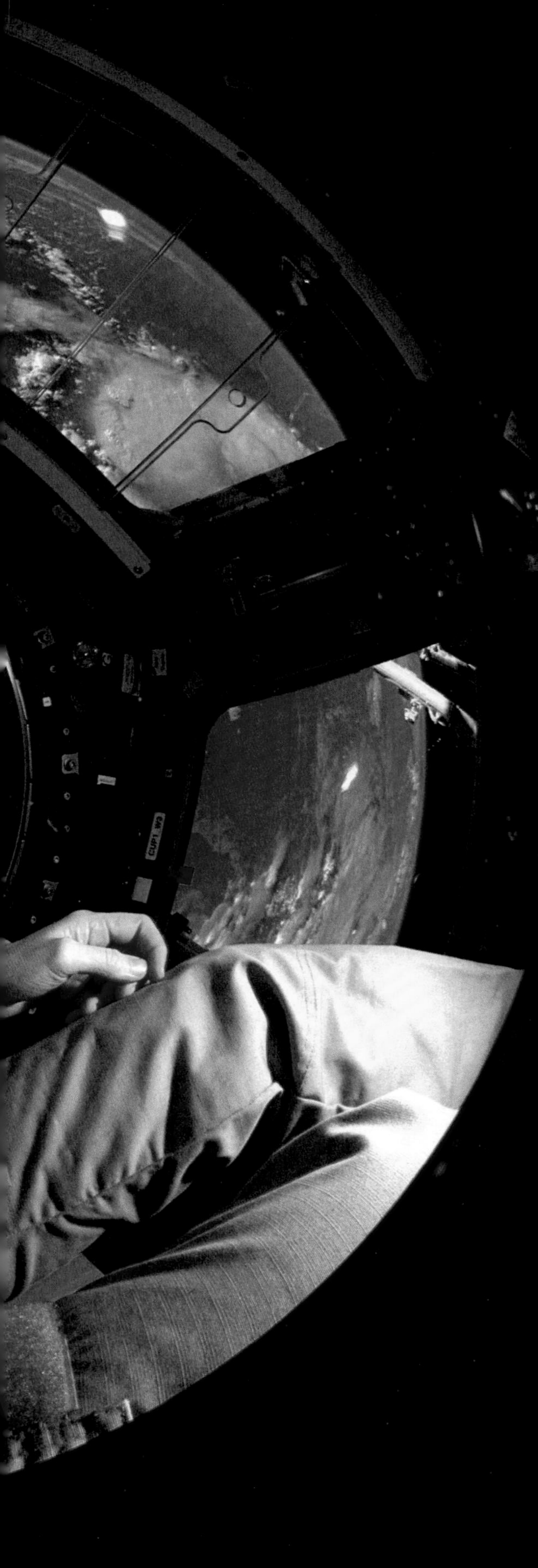

// A RECORD-BREAKING WOMAN

SAMANTHA CRISTOFORETTI
SHATTERS THE GLASS CEILING
BETWEEN EARTH AND ORBIT

◄ Cristoforetti, the first woman
to spend 200 days in space, enjoys
the view during her history-making
expedition. Her two "100 Days"
patches float in the background.

THERE'S NO SUCH THING AS A women's league in space. The U.S. may have won the Women's World Cup, and basketball may have the WNBA, but a WNASA never has been and never will be a thing. The boys' club that was space travel has long since become a co-ed enterprise. But that doesn't mean female astronauts and cosmonauts don't deserve to be recognized separately. With crews still predominantly male, there remains a glass ceiling between Earth and orbit, and it is the women, not the men, who must smash it. One of the most noteworthy of the current corps of female fliers is Italian fighter pilot Samantha Cristoforetti, who returned to Earth on June 11, 2015, after 200 days aboard the International Space Station, setting the women's duration record for time in space. Cristoforetti spoke to TIME in August to discuss her experiences in orbit, the challenges she faced there and the insights about life on Earth that come from being off it for so long. The interview has been edited for brevity and clarity.

TIME: Your recent stay on the ISS was your first trip to space. What surprised you most about your time there?
Cristoforetti: I don't think that I had very set expectations. I was very open, like a blank page. So I discovered many things, like how it feels to float—just that sensation of being so light to the point of having no weight whatsoever, of being able to move in three dimensions. Everything is just effortless. You're like Superman all day long for 200 days. But there, of course, are the challenges. You're used to setting things down and they're going to still be there when you go and get them. In space, if you just let something go, it's going to be gone. I got to the point, to the very advanced stage at the end of the mission, where I actually could let something just go, and I had just a subconscious awareness of what it was, and if it started to float away, I would just go and grab it.

With all the various ways of communicating with Earth when you're on the station, did you still feel any isolation?

In many ways, you still feel very connected because we are able to make phone calls to people on Earth. We have videoconferences scheduled on the weekends with our families. A selected number of people can send you emails, and we can email back and forth. We have kind of slow access to the Internet, and so we can do a little bit of social media and we can use the Internet if we are very patient. On the other hand, you also kind of live in a bubble because there's only so many people who actually have access to you. And then, of course, when you look at Earth, there's an ambivalent feeling because you know that you're not that far, but at the same time, it's such an alien view that you really feel like you're disconnected from the world. Everything flies by so fast that you almost don't have the time to make a virtual connection with whatever country or continent or feature is passing beneath you.

Did you feel you had any privacy while you were onboard?
The space station, first of all, is huge. Sometimes people think that we are like six people enclosed in very close quarters, in a very small environment. I attended a military academy

◀ Cristoforetti is all smiles as she rests up just minutes after landing in Zhezkazgan, Kazakhstan, on June 11, 2015. She had returned with crewmates Terry Virts and Anton Shkaplerov aboard the Soyuz TMA-15M spacecraft.

▼ The Soyuz TMA-15M undocks from the ISS; it brought Cristoforetti and her crewmates back to Earth in just a few hours.

when I was 24, and believe me, we were a lot more in closed quarters back then than I was in the space station. We also have a little bit of a personal space. It's about the size of an old phone booth, for people who are old enough to remember phone booths. You can close the doors. You sleep in there. It gets pretty dark. I had some pictures and other little personal items. And so definitely that's your private space, and most of us choose to go in there to make phone calls, for example, so that you don't disturb other people but also so that your phone call is private.

Now that you're the woman who holds the record for being in space the longest, how do you feel about your special status?
[*Laughs.*] Well, I think records are more something for media to write about because it's potentially a piece of news. But of course for me, it really doesn't make a huge difference having been in space 200 days as opposed to 190, which would not have been the record. I mean, I was happy to stay, but the opportunity to stay longer, which is what led to the record, depended on an accident that we had with [a Progress] cargo vehicle [which failed to reach orbit and delayed operations]. So really I didn't really do anything to earn that record.

You spent a couple of months with astronaut Scott Kelly and cosmonaut Misha Kornienko, who were aboard the station for a full year. What do you think was the hardest challenge they faced?
Well, you know, every person is different, so it's really hard to say what would be challenging for them. But I would imagine staying healthy. I felt, over the course of six months, my physical well-being somewhat degrading as time passed. It was nothing that I could really pinpoint but just the general sensation that my body over time was getting a little bit tired of this environment. I felt like my body probably at some point needed to get back to Earth, to breathing normal air, to be back in normal gravity.

Did your 200 days in space change your perspective about life on Earth?
When you look at the Earth from space, it looks like a big spaceship that is flying through space and oh, by the way, carrying all of humanity on it. And so you start to get this feeling that, just as on the space station, we can only function if we all work together as a crew and we're all crew members. None of us is a passenger. Nobody is up there because they bought a ticket and they're just going to enjoy the ride. You have to take care of each other. Now, it's a lot easier when it's six people, but we have to somehow progressively work toward having the same attitude on planet Earth. There's another crew coming afterward, the next generation, and we have to make sure that we'll leave them a spaceship which is in good shape.

// WATER WORLD

SCOTT KELLY TRAINS HIS CAMERA ON THE MAJESTIC BLUES OF THE EARTH'S SURFACE

Scott Kelly posted this image of Spain's coastline on a morning in August 2015.

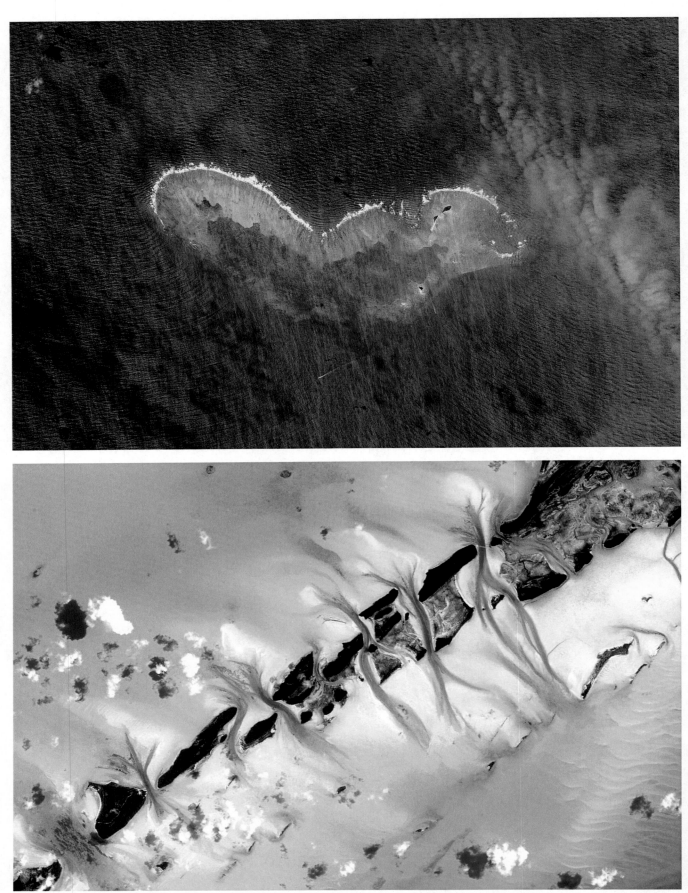

▲ Top: A butterfly-shaped formation in the Gulf of Mexico caught Kelly's eye in April 2015. Above: In a post about this image of the Bahamas, Kelly compared the shapes to strokes of watercolors. It was one of many photos he shared of the archipelago.

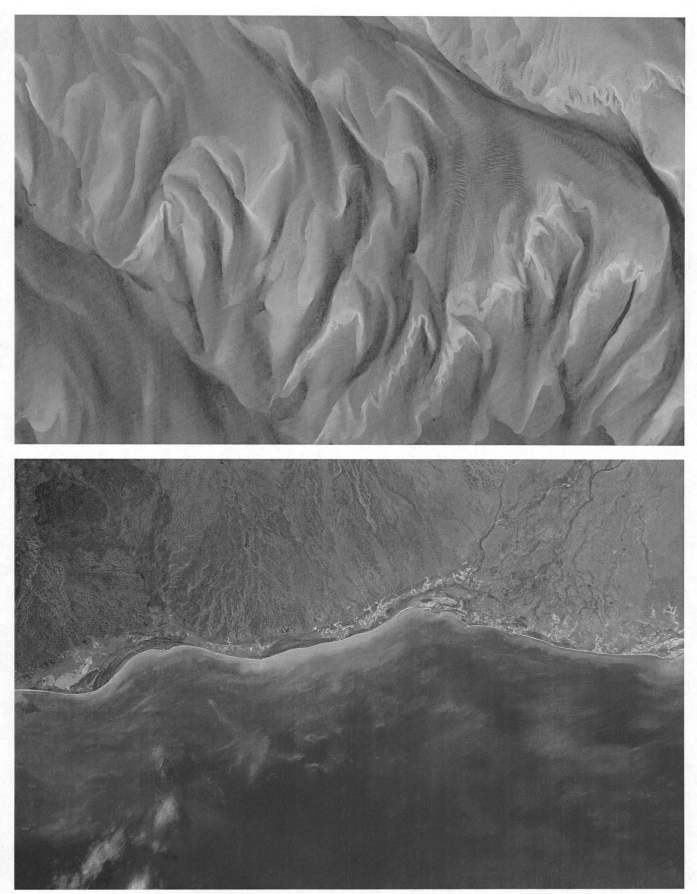

▲ Top: The waters of the Bahamas evoke mountain ranges in this shot, taken in January 2016.
Above: The Gulf of Carpentaria meets the rugged cliffs of Queensland, in Australia, in a May 2015 photo.

◀ In April 2015, during Kelly's first videoconference with his daughter Charlotte, he shared another image of the Bahamas.

// SHUTTLING SCIENCE

WHEN PERFORMED 250 MILES ABOVE THE EARTH, EVEN A SIMPLE BLOOD DRAW BECOMES COMPLEX

A Cygnus cargo vehicle, carrying supplies and research experiments, approaches the ISS's Canadarm2 as the robotic limb readies to capture the craft.

SCOTT KELLY IS SURELY THE ONLY astronaut in history who couldn't go to space without getting a tattoo first—two of them, in fact. You'd be hard-pressed to find Kelly's tats, and that's just how he wants it. There's one dot on his neck and one on his arm—and if they don't do much for body aesthetics, they've very valuable to science.

One of the tests Kelly and his crewmate Misha Kornienko were called upon to perform periodically was a sonogram of the carotid and brachial arteries to look for signs of atherosclerosis, the buildup of fatty plaques on arterial walls. The sonogram probes had to be placed just so, and it can take a long time for medics on the ground and astronauts in space to get the positioning right. So to save time, Kelly and a NASA sonographer visited a tattoo parlor on Earth, where the dots of ink were permanently applied at the right spots.

"He jokes those are the only tattoos he'll ever get," says Stuart Lee, the lead research scientist at the Johnson Space Center cardiovascular laboratory. "I tried to get him to get a larger tattoo that said PLACE PROBE HERE, but he didn't go for that idea."

For the researchers on Earth, the tattoos were a simple workaround to the challenge of monitoring subjects who were 250 miles overhead, spinning at more than 17,000 miles per hour. But other medical tasks proved more complex. Take blood sampling.

ISS crew members are trained at extracting one another's blood, but the proper lab facilities to analyze the samples are on the ground. The first step in getting them to where they need to go is to spin the blood in a centrifuge while it's still in space, which separates out its various components. The samples are then frozen until they can be packed aboard Soyuz spacecraft that periodically bring crew members home.

The moment a Soyuz thumps down in Kazakhstan, frozen scientific cargo is transferred to a Learjet and flown to Houston. The transfer time from space to Texas: 24 hours.

"It's unbelievable because it's faster than if you were on Earth and sending it to a clinical lab," says Andy Feinberg, the director of the Center for Epigenetics at Johns Hopkins University and one of the biomed researchers work-

THE MOMENT A SOYUZ THUMPS DOWN IN KAZAKHSTAN, FROZEN SCIENTIFIC CARGO IS TRANSFERRED TO A LEARJET AND FLOWN TO HOUSTON. TRANSFER TIME FROM SPACE TO TEXAS: 24 HOURS.

ing on the year-in-space mission. "This pushes the space mission, so it fits really well with how cutting-edge research labs work."

Studies of the microbiome—the ecosystem of bacteria, viruses, yeast and spores that populate the human gut—also rely on this kind of rapid shipment from space to lab. In this case, though, researchers relied on stool samples, which, while decidedly less glamorous, at least required less technical expertise to produce and store. The microbiomes of both Kelly brothers were studied this way over the year, with Scott eating a prescribed astronaut diet and Mark eating whatever he wanted. "Mark," says Scott Smith of the Nutritional Biochemistry Lab at the Johnson Space Center, "is free-range."

The research also has implications for people who never go into space—which is pretty much all of us. The microbiota's impact goes beyond the gut, says Fred Turek, a neurobiologist at Northwestern University and a researcher for the year-in-space mission. "It affects the cardiovascular system, bone density, even the brain. This could lead to research relating to psychological and neuropsychiatric disorders."

Studying the immune system takes its own kind of imagination. During long-duration space missions, the body's natural defenses can break down, partly because of oxidative and other metabolic stressors and partly because, in the controlled environment of a spacecraft, crew members are not exposed to all of the ambient organisms they would be on Earth. This may lead the immune system to let down its guard.

To help researchers compare how the Kelly brothers' immune systems function in differing environments, both brothers received flu vaccines before Scott went to space, and their responses were measured via blood samples. They were vaccinated again while Scott was in orbit and are scheduled to be so once more a year after his return.

"We take blood samples seven days after the vaccine because that's the peak time for cells recruited by the immune system to do their work," says Emmanuel Mignot of Stanford University, a mission scientist for the year-in-space project. "The risk exists that on a really long space mission, the immune system could unlearn immunities, so you could come back to Earth newly sensitive to pathogens."

Kelly and Kornienko's mission will not remotely answer all of the biomedical riddles space raises. Some of the answers may come only when human beings really do ship off for what would be a two-and-a-half-year mission to and from Mars. There is absolutely no guarantee that there won't be some nasty surprises waiting—some "knee in the curve," as space doctors say. But every day spent in space at the close remove of low-Earth orbit helps turn at least some of the unknowns into knowns.

ASTRONAUT KELLY'S DAUGHTER: MY DAD IS "OUT OF THIS WORLD"

Charlotte Kelly, the younger daughter of Scott Kelly, was a special TIME For Kids correspondent for the year. Charlotte turned 12 at the same moment her dad marked the halfway point of his year in space. Here were her thoughts at the time

IN A FEW DAYS I WILL HAVE REACHED THE SIX-month mark of seeing my dad off on his greatest adventure. Some might say that it is the ultimate adventure, but to my dad and our family, it's just another day of him at work.

You see, my dad is an out-of-this-world dad. Literally—he is out of this world. He is currently living and working aboard the International Space Station. Many of you know and hear about him as astronaut Scott Kelly, the American astronaut testing the limits of the human body living and working in space for one year.

To me, he is just Dad, and in a few days, I will turn 12, and my dad will mark his halfway point of his journey. We will celebrate by having dinner together via teleconference. It's not much, but it means the world to me.

I usually spend the better part of my summer break with my dad at his house. I could not stay at his place this summer, and I'm not so sure I would be up to it. It does look like fun floating around and spinning from one end of the space station to the next, but he works a lot, and I think I would have gotten in the way.

Summer did make the past three months go by pretty quickly, but the next three months will be a challenge. I will miss spending part of the holidays with my dad. This part is when having a dad with a cool job stinks.

// TIME FOR A WALK

SCOTT KELLY AND KJELL LINDGREN STEP OUTSIDE TO TACKLE MUCH-NEEDED UPGRADES TO THE SPACE STATION

A SPACECRAFT THAT KNOWS HOW TO repair or maintain itself hasn't been built yet. That's especially problematic when the one in question is the International Space Station—which is larger than a football field, weighs nearly 1 million pounds, and required more than 100 different spaceflights just to get its components into orbit and properly assembled. After 15 years of continuous occupancy, the ISS was in need of one of its periodic upgrades, and on November 6, astronauts and first-time spacewalkers Scott Kelly and Kjell Lindgren stepped outside for the first of two scheduled space walks to perform some much-needed work.

That space walk—or EVA (extravehicular activity), in NASA's preferred parlance—involved basic electrical work, with Kelly and Lindgren running new cables along parts of the station's length to provide power for docking ports that will be needed when new commercial crew and cargo vessels begin arriving in 2017. The astronauts also installed a thermal cover on a scien-

tific instrument to protect it from the extreme temperatures of space, and they lubricated portions of the ISS's robotic arm.

If that sounds like awfully undramatic, low-tech work, it's because it is. Build the most sophisticated machine you want, but it still comes down to the nuts-and-bolts business of, well, nuts and bolts. Doing basic handyman work is radically different in space, however—and radically more dangerous. In 2013 Italian astronaut Luca Parmitano nearly drowned during a space walk when coolant water leaked into his suit and began flooding his helmet.

To reduce the risks and help ensure that the necessary work gets done, many of the basic protocols for any space walk are worked out far in advance of a mission, with practice sessions in NASA's Neutral Buoyancy Lab (NBL), a 6.2-million-gallon swimming pool with a full-scale mock-up of much of the ISS resting on its bottom. But some of the details can't be fully validated until the astronauts are already in

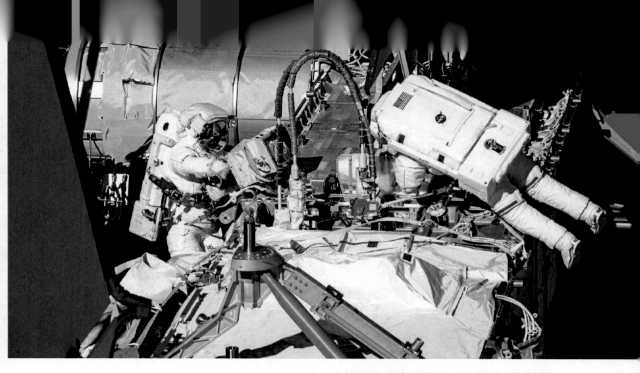

▲ Kjell Lindgren (in all white) and Kelly (with red stripes at his knees) work on the P6 Truss to open the Photovoltaic Radiator Fluid Quick Disconnect Coupling on Nov. 9, 2015.
◄ Scott Kelly takes his second space walk on Expedition 45.
► Kelly took this celebratory selfie on Oct. 28, 2015, during his first space walk. "Great first spacewalk yesterday," he later tweeted. "Now on to the next one next week."

space, which was true for Kelly, who went up far in advance of his scheduled walk.

Significant changes to the EVA plan are often beamed up to the crew first as simple PowerPoint-type animations. Finer points are worked out in the NBL and radioed up later in the most granular detail possible—the precise torque that has to be used to tighten a bolt and how many turns it will need before it's secure, for example. The determination of which man does which job while they're both outside is made by experience, skill set and a few other non-negotiable considerations.

Kelly, as the more senior of the two astronauts, was lead spacewalker for the first EVA, on October 28, which meant he was first out, last in, and generally in command throughout the exercise. His suit also had the red striping used to indicate the commander, which helps controllers identify who's who as they follow the exercise from the ground. Nonetheless, for that walk, Lindgren was assigned some of the more challenging work in

some of the trickier areas of the station. Why? "He has longer arms," says NASA's Grant Slusser, who was the ground director for the first EVA.

The mere business of getting the EVA suits ready can be a days-long job. Cooling loops that run through the garments like a human circulatory system have to be flushed with water to remove any contaminants. And while each suit is precisely tailored to the astronaut who will wear it, what fits on Earth may not fit in space, for the simple reason that without gravity, the spine may elongate a bit.

It's been more than half a century since cosmonaut Alexei Leonov became the first human being to walk in space, and in all that time the work hasn't gotten appreciably easier or safer. But it hasn't gotten less transcendent either. "You can hear your heart beat and you can hear yourself breathe," Leonov told photographer Marco Grob in a story for TIME. "Nothing else can accurately represent what it sounds like when a human being is in the middle of this abyss."

MAR
APR
MAY
JUN
JUL
AUG
SEPT
OCT
> NOV
DEC
JAN
FEB
MAR

// FIFTEEN YEARS AND...

*THE ASTRONAUTS CELEBRATE A MILESTONE
IN THE ORBITING STATION'S HISTORY*

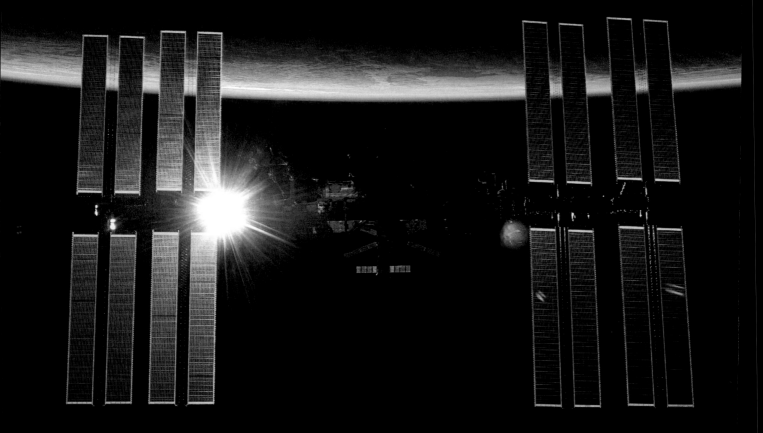

◄ A crew member of the space
shuttle *Endeavour* photographed
the ISS in May 2011.

YOU PROBABLY DON'T REMEMBER WHAT you were doing on Nov. 2, 2000, but astronaut Bill Shepherd and cosmonauts Yuri Gidzenko and Sergei Krikalev likely do. That was the day they climbed aboard the International Space Station, becoming its very first inhabitants—and beginning a streak for the station, which reached 15 straight years of occupancy last year.

Shepherd, Gidzenko and Krikalev—who were aboard for four months—were members of what was known as the Expedition 1 crew. Last December 15, Expedition 46, including Russian cosmonaut Yuri Malenchenko, American astronaut Tim Kopra and European Space Agency astronaut Tim Peake, lifted off to begin their own station stay.

In all, 221 people from 18 countries have lived aboard the ISS since 2000. During those 15 years, the station has made 87,600 revolutions around Earth, give or take the odd leap day. Oh, and in case anyone's counting, the crews have eaten approximately 25,000 meals—so far.

On the day the first crew climbed aboard, the ISS was little more than three pressurized modules, some supplies and a couple of solar wings to help keep it powered. Today the station is a flying piece of cosmic infrastructure, containing 15 pressurized modules, which afford the astronauts as much habitable space as a six-bedroom home. It weighs 1 million pounds, runs on 3.3 million lines of software code and required 115 launches just to carry all of its components up to orbit.

A lot has changed on Earth too in the past 15 years. When the station welcomed its first three visitors, Bill Clinton was rounding out the last few months of his presidency; Christina Aguilera's "Come on Over Baby (All I Want Is You)" topped the singles charts; *Meet the Parents* reigned at the box office; Miley Cyrus—who, history records, would later learn to twerk—was three weeks away from celebrating her eighth birthday; and the New York Mets had just lost the World Series, falling four games to one to the crosstown New York Yankees. (So some things haven't changed all that much.)

The fact that the space station exists at all is a testament not just to technology but to tenacity—and a little bit of wishful fantasy.

The project was first proposed in 1984 by President Ronald Reagan, who envisioned a completed space station, dubbed Freedom, going into service as early as 1988. That optimistic scenario was based on projections that the shuttles would prove to be such robust and reliable machines that one of them would be taking off every couple of weeks, making it not just easy to ship all of the necessary space station modules to orbit but affordable as well.

Even then, however, just three years after the first shuttle flew, the shuttles proved to be far more finicky and fragile than engineers had anticipated, with downtime between launches stretching from weeks to months. Two years later, in 1986, when the shuttle *Challenger* exploded on launch, the vision of shuttle as rugged delivery truck exploded with it.

At the same time, engineers looking at the plans for a space station with as many modules as Freedom called for were starting to get uneasy about the cost and complexity. America's only other space station, Skylab, launched in 1973, was just a single module built from a repurposed third stage of a Saturn V moon rocket. Russia's Salyut space stations were similar single-unit ships. The most complex station ever built before the ISS was Russia's Mir, consisting of seven pressurized modules, launched over the course of 10 years, and at the time *Challenger* exploded, none of those components had gotten off the ground. And here the U.S. was planning to fly a 15-module machine, relying on a launch vehicle that had just lost a crew.

All that caused the projected cost to soar and the entire plan to seem unrealistic. A solution presented itself in 1989, when the Soviet Union fell and the U.S. and Russia, once rivals in space, saw a way to cooperate. With that, the Freedom Space Station became the International Space Station—a global project that would include NASA and Roscosmos as senior partners and would eventually welcome 15 other nations or blocs, including Japan, Canada and the European Union, as collaborators. The first module may not have gone into space until a full 16 years after Reagan proposed the project, but the sprawling machine flying today is proof that the result has been worth the wait.

// THE INTERNATIONAL SPACE STATION BY THE NUMBERS

THE INTERNATIONAL SPACE STATION IS ABOUT THE SIZE OF AN AMERICAN FOOTBALL STADIUM

MODULE LENGTH 167.3 FEET
TRUSS LENGTH 357.5 FEET
SOLAR ARRAY LENGTH 239.4 FEET
MASS 924,739 POUNDS
HABITABLE VOLUME 13,696 CUBIC FEET
PRESSURIZED VOLUME 32,333 CUBIC FEET
POWER GENERATION 8 SOLAR ARRAYS = 84 KILOWATTS

LIVING AND WORKING IN ORBIT ON THE INTERNATIONAL SPACE STATION

Crews have eaten about **25,000 MEALS** since the first crew's arrival in 2000

Approximately **7 TONS OF SUPPLIES** support a crew of 3 for about **6 MONTHS**

Astronauts and cosmonauts have spent more than **1,000 HOURS** aboard the spacecraft

Within and outside the station, more than **1,500** scientific investigations have been performed

ONE THING YOU CAN SAY ABOUT THE INTERNATIONAL SPACE STATION . . .

It's big—larger than a **6-BEDROOM HOUSE**

Has the internal volume of a **BOEING 747**

Weighs almost a million pounds (equivalent to more than **320 AUTOMOBILES**)

Travels a distance equivalent **TO THE MOON AND BACK** in about a day

THE INTERNATIONAL SPACE STATION

is a global program visited by more than 200 people from 15 nations

NASA U.S.

ROSCOSMOS RUSSIA

CSA ASC CANADA

esa EUROPE

JAXA JAPAN

INTERNATIONAL SPACE STATION TIMELINE

It was November 1998 when the first modules for the space station were carried into orbit. Back on Earth, Google was brand-new and the iPod was still three years away

NOV. 20, 1998
First module: Russian Zarya

DEC. 6, 1998
First U.S module: Unity

OCT. 30, 2000
First crew: Expedition 1

NOV. 30, 2000
First U.S. solar arrays

FEB. 7, 2001
First U.S. lab: Destiny

FEB. 7, 2008
First European module: Columbus

MAR. 11, 2008
First component of Japanese Kibo module

MAR. 15, 2009
Final solar arrays

FEB. 24, 2011
Final module assembly complete: Italian Leonardo

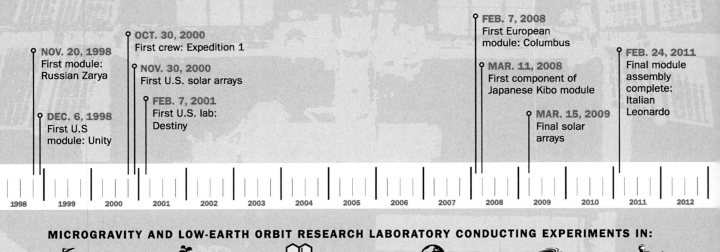

1998 | 1999 | 2000 | 2001 | 2002 | 2003 | 2004 | 2005 | 2006 | 2007 | 2008 | 2009 | 2010 | 2011 | 2012

MICROGRAVITY AND LOW-EARTH ORBIT RESEARCH LABORATORY CONDUCTING EXPERIMENTS IN:

HUMAN RESEARCH / LIFE SCIENCES / PHYSICAL SCIENCES / EARTH SCIENCES / ASTROPHYSICS / TECHNOLOGY

THE LONGEST TRIP
Scott Kelly holds the world's title . . . for now
BY JONATHAN D. WOODS

EXACTLY 216 DAYS AFTER NASA ASTRONAUT SCOTT Kelly strapped into a Soyuz rocket in the middle of the Kazakh desert, he broke the record for the longest single stay in space by an American astronaut. The record had previously been held by Spanish-American astronaut Michael López-Alegría, who spent 215 days in orbit in 2007. (Soviet cosmonaut Valeri Polyakov holds the overall record of 437 continuous days in 1994 and 1995.)

From the time Kelly got to space on March 28, 2015, until the time he came home on March 2, 2016—logging a total of 340 days aloft—he sped around Earth once every 88 minutes, or 16 times every day, aboard the International Space Station. "I kinda forgot what it's like to live down there" (that is, Earth), says Kelly of his record-breaking stay.

Space travel is not supposed to be about bragging rights, as Italian astronaut Samantha Cristoforetti insisted when she set the record for the longest stay by a female astronaut, at 200 days. But what space is supposed to be about and what it is about are often two different things, and from the moment Yuri Gagarin became the first human being in orbit on April 12, 1961, astronauts have been competing (sometimes quietly, sometimes not) to go higher, faster and farther.

Kelly knows his record can't stand forever—and Polyakov's can't either—if human beings are ever going to make the two-and-a-half-year journey to Mars and back. And that's how it should be. There was a time, after all, that America's great space marathoner was Gordon Cooper, who went aloft in a Mercury spacecraft in 1963. His record stay in low-Earth orbit: 33 hours.

THE HEARTBREAKING LOSS
OF TWO CARGO SHIPS

*A Russian Progress spacecraft and a SpaceX rocket from
the U.S. are destroyed in confidence-shaking accidents*

THERE ARE UNCOUNTABLE LAWS OF physics and engineering that govern the launch of a rocket. But there's one that supersedes all the others: ultimately, stuff will blow up. Always has, always will.

That rule played out in a dramatic way in mid-2015 when successive cargo ships destined for the ISS failed—one when a Russian spacecraft lost contact with Earth and spun helplessly out of control while in orbit, the other in a fiery U.S. launch accident that occurred only seconds after liftoff. The episodes did not pose a threat to the ISS crew and did not suggest that those aboard the station were in danger of running out of water, food or breathable oxygen. But the dispiriting loss of the two craft, which cost millions of dollars and untold man-hours, reminded the world of the real and grave risks posed by space exploration.

The first accident involved a Russian Progress cargo vehicle that was launched atop a Soyuz rocket on April 28 from the Baikonur Cosmodrome in Kazakhstan. The ship carried three tons of supplies, including propellant, oxygen, water, spare parts, crew clothing and space-walk hardware, and a replica of the Soviet victory banner that had been raised above the German Reichstag in 1945 at the end of World War II. The vehicle quickly reached orbit as planned, but what followed was something else entirely. Within hours, the Progress began what NASA at first dubbed a "slow spin." From there, trouble accelerated, ending with the vehicle plunging back through the atmosphere, incinerating itself and its cargo.

Following the Progress explosion came the even more disappointing June 2015 loss of a U.S.-made Falcon 9 rocket and unmanned Dragon cargo vehicle. Built by Elon Musk's California-based Space Exploration Technologies Corporation (SpaceX), the rocket and cargo ship launched at 10:21 a.m. on June 28 from Cape Canaveral, Fla. The rocket came undone before its first stage had even shut down and separated, then blew itself to pieces and settled into the Atlantic just

◀ Opposite: The Falcon 9 rocket and Dragon cargo vehicle launch at 10:21 a.m. on June 28, 2015. ▲ Above, from left: Shortly after its liftoff, the Falcon 9 rocket breaks apart, losing an International Docking Adapter in the accident; Scott Kelly's view of Cape Canaveral following the Falcon 9 explosion. ▶ On Aug. 24, 2015, Japan's Kounotori 5 H-II Transfer Vehicle makes its final approach toward the ISS carrying more than 4.5 tons of cargo.

off the Cape Canaveral coast. The disaster not only cost the ISS crew needed supplies, it also shook confidence in SpaceX, a NASA partner in building rockets and spacecraft to conduct long-term work in space.

The key piece of cargo carried by the Dragon was an International Docking Adapter (IDA) designed to connect to an ISS module and serve as an attachment node for private crew vehicles scheduled to begin flying in 2017. Without the IDA, it was unclear how far ISS crew members would get in reconfiguring the ISS's modules in advance of the arrival of the new crew vehicles. Musk, the entrepreneurial founder of SpaceX, took to Twitter to acknowledge the debacle. Scott Kelly, then in his third month of his marathon year aboard the ISS, expressed his dismay via social media as well: "Watched #Dragon launch from @space_station Sadly failed Space is hard." NASA, too, said it was "disappointed" by the loss of the mission.

It was later determined that a broken two-foot-long piece of steel, called a strut, caused the accident, and eventually SpaceX recovered the first stage of the Falcon 9 rocket, which had landed upright just six miles from the launch site. That was crucial, because the purpose of the rocket, in addition to resupplying the ISS, was to recover

the Falcon 9 so SpaceX could reuse it to decrease the cost of future missions.

Fortunately, the failures were followed by delivery success stories. In July 2015, an unmanned Progress 60 Russian resupply craft, carrying 106 pounds of oxygen, 926 pounds of water, 1,940 pounds of propellant and 3,133 pounds of space parts, docked at the ISS. The arrival of the gear prompted celebration. "Christmas in July!" the astronauts announced in a tweet.

The capper came in August when a 164-foot rocket built by the Japanese Aerospace Exploration Agency scored a second delivery. The ship, the H-II, ferried 4.5 tons of cargo, including a processing unit for purifying and recycling urine and an experiment called the Calorimetric Electron Telescope for the study of cosmic radiation.

The most charming entries on the flight manifest: 14 miniature satellites known as cubesats, built by the San Francisco–based company Planet Labs. Once deployed, the satellites were designed to beam down high-resolution images of Earth to paying customers. But since "cubesat" lacked a certain lyricism, Planet Labs chose to call the little satellites Doves.

Space may be hard—sometimes too hard— but on August 24, the Doves arrived safely.

// CITIES FROM ABOVE

A DIFFERENT PERSPECTIVE ON FAMILIAR TERRAIN, FROM SHANGHAI TO HOUSTON

▶ Scott Kelly tweeted this shot of San Francisco exactly a month after his liftoff to the ISS.

◄ This nightscape of Shanghai was taken on Feb. 6, 2015—the Chinese New Year and Kelly's 318th day in space.

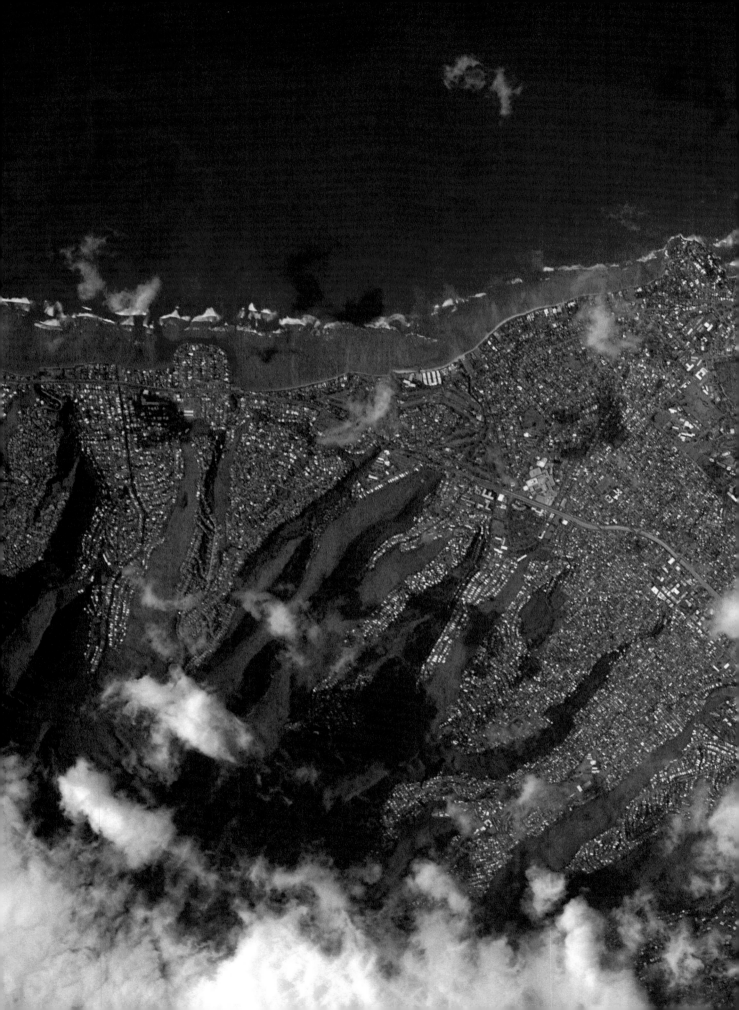

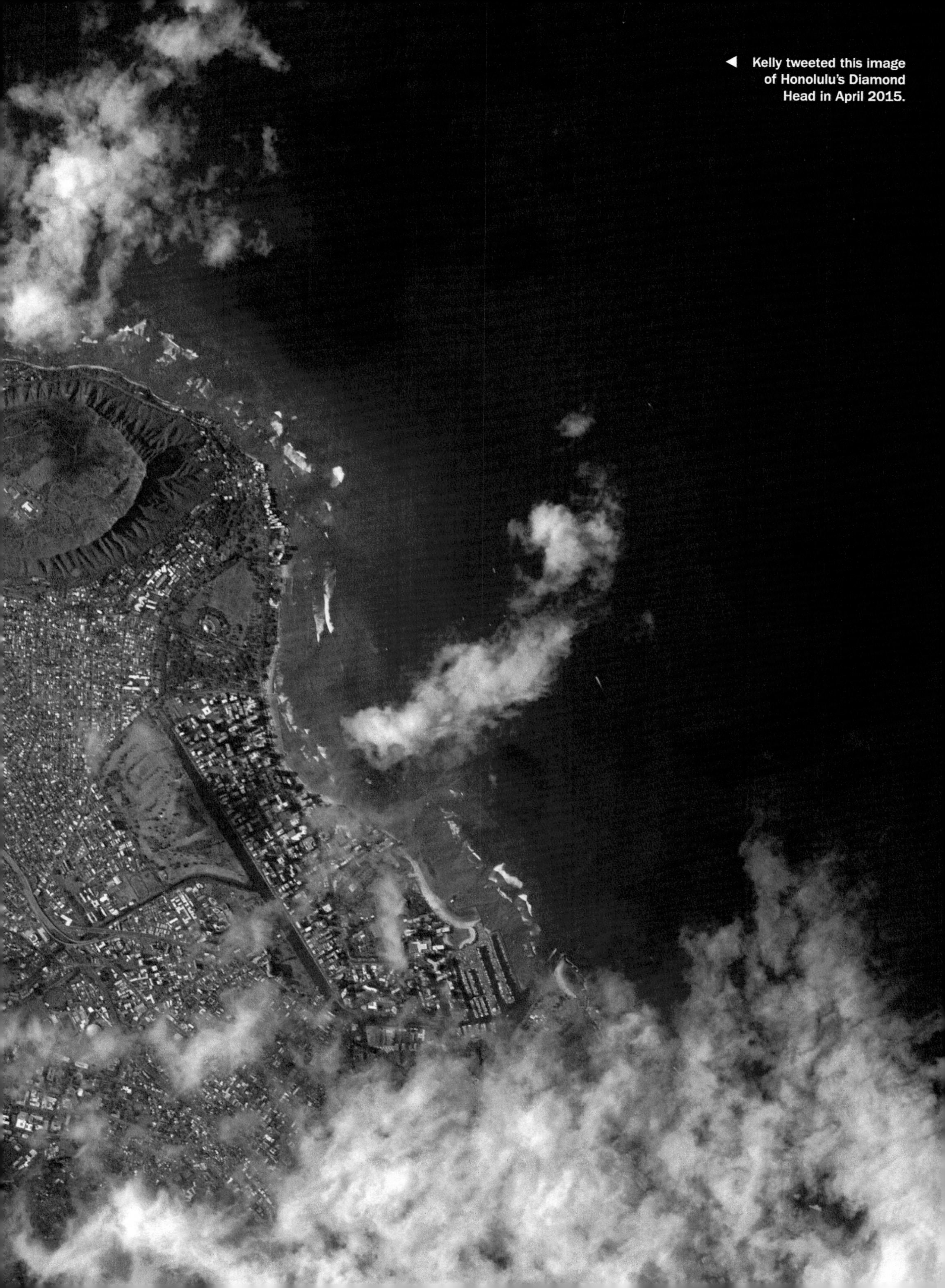

◀ Kelly tweeted this image of Honolulu's Diamond Head in April 2015.

// EMERGENCY SPACE WALK

IN A DRAMATIC MOMENT, COMMANDER KELLY AND ASTRONAUT TIM KOPRA REPAIR A STUCK ROBOTIC ARM

▲ Astronaut Tim Kopra experiences the joy—and challenge—of a space walk on Dec. 21, 2015. Kelly reminded him not to go back inside without taking time to appreciate the view.

▲ The Japan Aerospace Exploration Agency Kounotori 5 HTV-F is seen here over the illuminated Nile River on Earth.
▶ On Dec. 21, 2015, commander Scott Kelly (pictured here) and flight engineer Tim Kopra successfully move the ISS's mobile transporter railcar to prepare for the arrival of a Russian cargo-supply spacecraft.

THE INTERNATIONAL SPACE STATION had a rough go of it in 2015, with no fewer than three accidents or anomalies occurring during launch that prevented cargo vehicles from getting to orbit. In December 2015, another problem aboard the ISS itself threatened to prevent the vehicles that do get to space from actually docking with the station—and one of those vehicles was poised to launch. That necessitated an emergency space walk by commander Scott Kelly and astronaut Tim Kopra.

The problem involved the space station's robotic arm, which moves from place to place along the station's central truss aboard a sort of miniature railcar. When an uncrewed cargo vehicle arrives, it's the job of the arm to reach out and grab it, then ease it in for a docking. But during one routine run along the truss, the arm got stuck just four inches from where it needed to be to grapple an incoming ship.

"The Mobile Transporter railcar on the truss was being moved by robotic flight controllers to worksite 4 when it stopped moving," NASA spokesman Rob Navias told TIME in an email. "Cause is still being evaluated, but might be a stuck brake handle."

That came at a very bad time. Just three days later, the Progress 62 cargo vehicle was scheduled to launch from Baikonur, Kazakhstan, in preparation for a docking with the station. NASA and the Russians faced the twin dramas

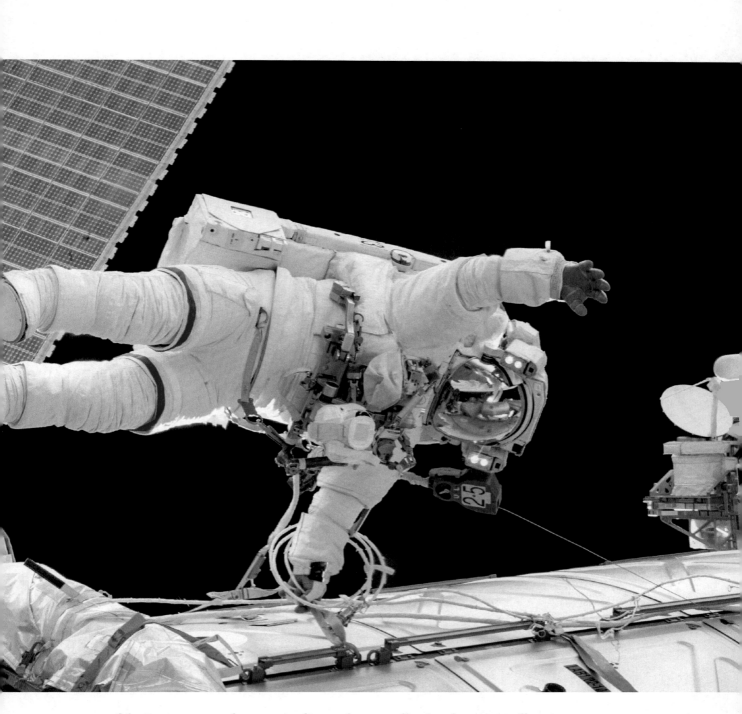

of the Progress countdown proceeding at the same time Kelly and Kopra were preparing to fix the transporter car—and they managed the crisis deftly.

Less than four hours after the Progress vehicle—loaded with 5,753 pounds of cargo—lifted off, Kelly and Kopra were suiting up and heading out. Once on the truss, they made quick work of the problem. Kelly gave the brake handle a couple of swift hits, disengaging it and

allowing the arm to roll again.

"It's moving now," he radioed to the ground. "I hit it twice; I think that fixed it. That was pretty easy."

Actually, *easy* does not describe it. The space walk took more than three hours for a job that on the ground would take a few seconds. But there were compensations. "Make sure you look at the Earth," Kelly reminded Kopra. That, as much as anything, made the hard work worth it.

// EARTH LINK

WITH A CONSTANT STREAM OF PHOTOGRAPHS, HUMOROUS HASHTAGS, SELFIES AND VIDEO FOOTAGE, KELLY KEPT HIS FOLLOWERS UP TO DATE VIA TWITTER, INSTAGRAM AND FACEBOOK

Scott Kelly @StationCDRKelly • 26 Mar 2015
Enjoying a moment of solitude before my
#YearInSpace.

Scott Kelly @StationCDRKelly • 12 Jul 2015
#bahamas and me. I think we all know who's better looking
#YearInSpace

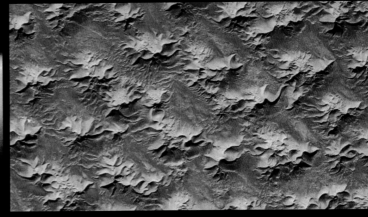

Scott Kelly @StationCDRKelly • 29 Jul 2015
#EarthArt The color psychology of orange is optimistic. From my view
things are looking up down there. #YearInSpace

Scott Kelly @StationCDRKelly • 26 Jul 2015
Caught these high altitude clouds over the Pacific. Wow!
#YearInSpace

Scott Kelly @StationCDRKelly • 5 Apr 2015
The #EasterBunny came to visit! #HappyEaster from #ISS.
#YearInSpace

Scott Kelly @StationCDRKelly • 19 May 2015
@POTUS Welcome to @Twitter, Mr. President. You told me to #IG
my mission up here Glad to see you tweeting down there

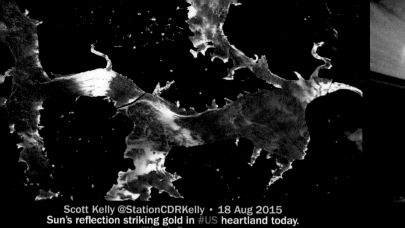

Scott Kelly @StationCDRKelly • 18 Aug 2015
Sun's reflection striking gold in #US heartland today.
#YearInSpace

Scott Kelly @StationCDRKelly • 28 Aug 2015
#Aurora seen in a new light with a different camera lens.
#YearInSpace

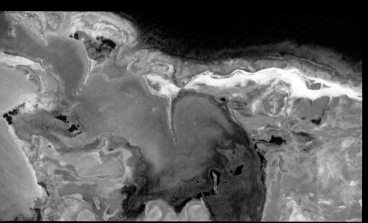

Scott Kelly @StationCDRKelly • 16 Sep 2015
#EarthArt Half a year, still she dazzles, colors, intrigues, excites, amuses
interests and shines. #YearInSpace

Scott Kelly @StationCDRKelly • 23 Oct 2015
Hurricane #Patricia approaches #Mexico It's massive. Be careful!
#YearInSpace

Scott Kelly @StationCDRKelly • 9 Aug 2015
Day 135 #MilkyWay You're old, dusty, gassy and warped. But beautiful.
Good from the @space_station #YearInSpace

Scott Kelly @StationCDRKelly • 23 Dec 2015
Our plants aren't looking too good. Would be a problem on Mars.
I'm going to have to channel my inner Mark Watney.

Scott Kelly @StationCDRKelly • 11 Dec 2015
They arrived in space like baby birds barely able to fly & now they soar
home as eagles. Great job Kjell and Kimiya!

Scott Kelly @StationCDRKelly • 5 Feb 2016
Honor to talk to President George H.W. Bush today from
@Space_Station! Thank you for visiting our great NASA team!

// THE SEARCH FOR LIFE

EVEN BEFORE WE FIND AN ORGANISM,
THE DEBATE MAY BE SETTLED

▶ The Pillars of Creation, columns of interstellar gas
in the Eagle Nebula that were captured by NASA's
Hubble Space Telescope, are about five light-years tall.

F YOU ASK NICELY, SCOTT SANDFORD will build you a piece of the universe. It won't be a big piece; that'd be way too much for a single astrobiologist in a single lab at the NASA Ames Research Center near Silicon Valley. And it won't be a very interesting piece—just the gas and dust of interstellar space. He'll swirl it all together in a little chamber in a big machine and chill it down to 40 Kelvins, which is –388°F and, no matter what you call it, is very, very cold. "You're not allowed to put your tongue on that," he says, pointing to the chamber.

Then he does a very important thing: he hits the gas and dust with radiation—all kinds of radiation, as long as it's the kind you'd find in space. And right then, everything changes.

"You get enormous chemical diversity," he says. "We get thousands if not tens of thousands of products. Some of these are more stable than others. And some are molecules like amino acids: stuff that life uses."

How did we—humanity, that is—get here? From the point of view of science, like it or not, the common chemical soup in Sandford's lab is all there is to it. Our growing appreciation of that is just the latest step in a long process of human humbling. Earth was the center of the universe once, until it wasn't. Our solar system, at least, was the most important place in the galaxy—but that turned out not to be so either. And the Milky Way itself is only one of at least 100 billion galaxies.

Finally, though, there was life: the animation of an entire planet with things that walk and crawl and fly and swim and, in the case of human beings, think big thoughts. Surely that was the longest of long shots, something unique to the sole world with exactly the right mix of ingredients, orbiting exactly the right distance from exactly the right star. Just look around you: if life is out there, where is it?

That hasn't stopped people from looking, of course. For a long time, the search for life had been a more or less passive exercise: scan the skies for signals from another civilization, chop into space rocks that happen to fall on us, or wait—if you believe in such things—for aliens to land and settle the question once and for all. But in recent years the science has gotten much more serious and much more rigorous. The SETI (Search for Extraterrestrial Intelligence) Institute, in Mountain View, Calif., not far from NASA Ames, is expanding its work beyond just listening for signals from space to looking for optical clues like laser flashes. Other researchers want to hunt for traces of biology such as methane and carbon dioxide in the atmosphere of alien worlds.

But the most compelling work is being done in labs like Sandford's, where researchers are trying to determine not just whether extraterrestrial life exists but what it would look like and how it would function. Animating this new push for answers is the growing belief among many scientists that the question of whether alien life exists at all is an outdated one. Life is out there, all right, simply because it has to be. Water, which is indispensable for biology as we know it, is one of the most common compounds in the cosmos. Amino acids routinely turn up in the meteorites that have been analyzed. And while as recently as 20 years ago we knew of no other planets in the universe apart from the handful in our own solar system, we've since spotted thousands of possible or confirmed worlds circling other stars.

As humanity moves ever closer to a trip to Mars to hunt for life—and as American astronaut Scott Kelly wraps up a year aboard the International Space Station to help prove that the human body can survive the rigors of so long a stretch in zero-G—it seems more and more that so ambitious a journey is very much worth making. Life on other worlds may be not only possible, not only likely, but chemically and mathematically inevitable. "The universe is hardwired to be an organic chemist," says Sandford. "It's not a very clean or tidy one, but it has really big beakers and plenty of time."

NEW RESEARCH SUGGESTS THAT COSMIC BIOLOGY IS NOT JUST POSSIBLE; IT'S INEVITABLE.

It is NASA Ames that is conducting the world's most comprehensive search for life in space, coordinating its work with that of eight universities as well as the SETI. The likelihood of any such researchers' actually finding evidence of life in space—specifically, intelligent life in our own galaxy with which we could communicate—was first formulated by astronomer Frank Drake, in 1961, with his namesake Drake equation.

Drake's formula begins with the rate of formation of stars that could support habitable worlds, then multiplies that figure by the fraction of those stars that have planets, and further by the fraction of those planets that are suitable for life, the fraction on which life actually appears, and so on down for a few more multipliers, including the share of that life that becomes intelligent. The final tally of extraterrestrial civilizations you wind up with depends on how you fill in those Xs—which depends at least partly on how optimistic you are. Drake has estimated the figure to be 10,000 worlds. Carl Sagan put it at 1 million.

"As long as none of the factors are zero," says Sandford, "you'd expect there to be life."

The risk of getting stuck with a zero went down in 2009, after the launch of the planet-hunting Kepler space telescope. Kepler's job was a simple one: to stare at a fixed patch of space, looking for the subtle dimming of light around a star when an orbiting planet passes in front of it. That change would be tiny—"If a star is 10,000 lightbulbs, the transit of an Earth-like planet is like taking one bulb away," says Natalie Batalha, a NASA astrophysicist and the Kepler mission scientist.

Still, in the brief time Kepler has been operating, it has discovered 4,706 candidate planets, of which 1,039 have been confirmed. Making that figure more impressive, all of these worlds have been found in a very small patch of sky, just 3,000 light-years deep—or about 3% of the depth of the Milky Way—and just 10 degrees by 10 degrees across the entire canopy of the sky. "It's like the size of my open palm held at arm's length," says Batalha.

That's an embarrassment of planetary riches, but if you're looking for life, you can narrow the field some. First, your planet needs to be

> ## "THE UNIVERSE IS HARDWIRED TO BE AN ORGANIC CHEMIST. IT'S NOT A VERY CLEAN OR TIDY ONE, BUT IT HAS REALLY BIG BEAKERS AND PLENTY OF TIME."
>
> —SCOTT SANDFORD, NASA ASTROBIOLOGIST

orbiting its parent sun in the so-called Goldilocks zone: the not-too-hot, not-too-cold place where liquid water can exist. It should also be a relatively small world, from one Earth radius up to about two Earth radii in size. Those are the places likely to have both a rocky surface and enough gravity to hold onto their atmosphere, assuming they have one in the first place. Once you have a world like that, just add some water, season with hydrocarbons, wait a billion years or so, and hello, ET. Sure, that might overstate it, but not by too much.

"Life on Earth got started very quickly," says SETI senior astronomer Seth Shostak. "That's like walking into a casino in Vegas, pulling the handle and winning the jackpot. You say, 'Well, either I'm very, very lucky or this is not a difficult bet.'"

Shostak is decidedly on the side of its not being a difficult bet, and Sandford's work at NASA is helping to make that case. Much of Sandford's research involves what are known as amphiphiles, hydrocarbon chains that make up our cell walls. One end of the chain is hydrophilic (it loves water); the other end is lipophilic (it hates water but loves fat). No sooner do amphiphiles start forming in a preorganic world—which is easy enough to do as atoms link up into stable molecules—than the chains solve the problem of their bipolar nature by gathering into membranes with the ends that like water on the outside and the ends that like fat on the inside.

Over time, the membranes get bigger, and if they happen to incorporate molecules that make them resistant to excessive ultraviolet radiation, which can damage cells, and to survive in a range of acidities, the hardier little membranes eventually crowd out the more fragile ones. It's not life, but it's a good start.

"You have to go through a phase where everything is largely driven by the chemical nature of things," says Sandford. "[But] since the laws of physics and chemistry are the same everywhere, if you have similar starting components and similar environments, you should get similar outcomes."

But the next step toward life is a big one: an incipient organism must develop an information-storage system, which on Earth is RNA and DNA. That's a chemical trick that is many orders of magnitude more complicated than growing a membrane, but it's an indispensable criterion for life. Says NASA planetary scientist Chris McKay, "A hurricane is a self-organizing, self-propagating system with a life cycle. It's born, it grows, it eats, and then it dies. Why isn't it alive?"

The answer, in this view, is that it can't remember what it's doing or how it's changed and pass those improvements on. The easiest answer to how an information-storage system gets started would come through a modern-day analogue to the celebrated Miller-Urey experiment, the 1953 study in which two University of Chicago researchers re-created what they believed to be the atmospheric conditions on the early Earth and shot electricity through the model—representing lightning—which produced hydrocarbons. It was the precursor to Sandford's much more complex studies and offered a satisfyingly simple deus ex machina by which prebiotic chemistry could have taken a big jump.

A far more complicated and theoretical answer could come through the head-spinning world of quantum physics, which demolishes our familiar concept of linear time and allows it to bend back in sort of a repeating loop. That, argues McKay, means life might effectively program itself, with the mature organisms that exist at the end of an evolutionary line writing the code for the rudimentary organisms that exist at the beginning, which then grow up and become the code writers themselves. "I'm not saying it's a mature idea or thought," he says. "I'm saying that we are so young in our appreciation of things that it would be hard to rule out anything."

It's also possible that we don't have to limit our search to life as we know it, because there could be uncountable kinds of life as we *don't* know it. The most commonly posited examples of alternative biology are organisms that are not carbon-based, like we are, but silicon-based. Silicon and carbon are close neighbors on the periodic table, and both bond easily with other elements. But silicon doesn't play well with water, which acts as the critical solvent in all forms of life we understand. "In silicon chemistry, a lot of the things we use in our biology would explode or combust in water," says Tori Hoehler, a NASA chemist and biologist.

Methane is the next-best guess for a solvent, and silicon does behave better in that medium. Saturn's moon Titan is known to have lakes of ethane and methane, which is why the *Cassini* orbiter dropped a probe into Titan's atmosphere to study its chemistry when it arrived in the Saturnian system in 2004. And while liquid methane is cold—on the order of −258°F—nothing says that other forms of life have to be happy at what we think of as room temperature. Maybe their rooms are just really, really cold.

Still, life as we know it—warm, watery and carbon-based—might remain the best model. Chemistry and evolution are both, in their own ways, lazy. They take the simplest routes to elegant solutions. Perhaps there are other ways to get the biological job done, but it's hard to come up with a better alternative.

Ultimately, as many astrobiologists argue, the question of life in space might be as simple as a three-part formula: chemistry plus energy plus time. McKay likes to cite what's known as the zero-one-infinity rule, which applies in a lot of scientific theories but especially in the search for life. We know that the number of planets in the universe with life is not zero. We know so far that it's at least one. If we do find another, it makes no chemical or mathematical sense for the total potential figure not to be unlimited.

"So what we're searching for," says McKay, "is two." That search is as big as the universe—but so is the promise it holds.

MAR

APR

MAY

JUN

JUL

AUG

SEPT

OCT

NOV

DEC

JAN

FEB

> MAR

// HOMECOMING

WITH THE WORLD WATCHING, SCOTT KELLY, MIKHAIL KORNIENKO AND SERGEY VOLKOV MADE A PICTURE-PERFECT TOUCHDOWN IN KAZAKHSTAN ON MARCH 2

◀ Expedition 46 touches down southeast of the town of Dzhezkazgan in Kazakhstan.

DATES, RAISINS AND SWEETENED DOUGH would surely look good to a space-station crew member who has just put in the average six-month hitch in orbit—to say nothing of Scott Kelly and Mikhail Kornienko after nearly a full year. But it would take a brave astronaut to eat the dates, raisins and sweetened dough they served up during the welcome-home ceremony at Zhezkazgan Airport in Kazakhstan.

That's because what an astronaut's stomach says and what an astronaut's otoliths say are two different things. And when you're back on Earth and feeling the tug of gravity after a long period in weightlessness, it's the otoliths—the little stones of floating calcium in the inner ear that govern balance and prevent motion sickness—that rule.

For that reason, nobody ate a bite as Kelly, Kornienko and Russian cosmonaut Sergey Volkov, who only two hours earlier had landed in the steppe in their Soyuz spacecraft, were helped to their chairs in the airport receiving area. While Kazakh, Russian and American dignitaries applauded, a fusillade of cameras flashed and four young women in traditional Kazakh costume—long, bright, yellow-and-green dresses with bright green headpieces—brought in the traditional foods.

There were other gifts, too, for the men who had begun their day 250 miles overhead, circling the planet once every 88 minutes. There was a medal for Volkov, who had commanded the spacecraft on its return. There were Russian nesting dolls with the likeness of each astronaut painted on the front.

And for Kelly, who has now flown four missions and holds the American record for longest unbroken stay in space, there was the inevitable question: "Would you consider going back?"

His answer was succinct. "I would always consider flying in space," he said, "no question."

That may just be astronaut bravado, though you wouldn't have known it to look at Kelly. Volkov entered the room at the airport with the telltale gait of a person just back from space—back straight, head upright, eyes locked ahead. He dared not turn to look at someone without rotating his entire body, since pivoting his head—or, much worse, flicking his eyes—would

bring on a dizzy, sickly swoon. Kornienko looked better, though he was drawn and clearly fatigued.

Kelly, however, nodded, turned, smiled and joked and looked every bit like a man who had spent the past 340 days on Earth, not circling and circling above it. "What's with all the overcoats?" he asked the rescuers who extracted him from the capsule in the frigid wind of the frozen steppe. "This feels great."

Aches and pains kicked in a few days later, but they could not detract from the initial exhilaration of returning safely from a year in space. The entire process of rescuing a Soyuz crew is an act of human caretaking on a massive scale. It takes a month of planning, the coordination of three countries, and the chessboard-like deployment of three separate teams of helicopters, all-terrain vehicles, snowmobiles and rescuers in a great triangle in northern Kazakhstan bounded by the cities of Karaganda, Zhezkazgan and Arkalyk. Poor weather in one corner of the vast field would mean shifting part of the deployment to another. A shallow—or ballistic—reentry would have meant sprinting far south of all three cities for an emergency rescue at a less-certain site.

That job completed, next will come the bio-

▲ Top left: the arrival of the Soyuz TMA-18M on March 2, 2016. Top right: the landing site as viewed through the window of a Russian MI-8 helicopter arriving on the scene.
◀ Near left: commander Kelly rests after a safe landing at 10:26 a.m. local time. "What's with all the overcoats?" Kelly asked the rescuers. "This feels great."

medical work that was the entire purpose of the mission. The more times astronauts go to space, the better they adapt to the otherworldly state of zero-G and readapt to the leaden feel of a gravity field when they return, which helped explain Kelly's apparent ease in the airport.

But the physical insults of space travel—the toll weightlessness takes on all of the body's systems, not to mention the damage the constant bath of high radiation can do to the DNA—may be cumulative. A lone week in space could do much less damage than an additional week heaped on top of the 49 Kelly spent there.

The great twins experiment, with Kelly's brother Mark serving as a genetically identical control subject, will help scientists determine which of the changes that Scott's body underwent in the past year are indeed attributable to his time in orbit and which are the result of nothing more than a 51-year-old man living the year that turns him 52.

Finding those answers will be critical to discovering whether human beings, who brashly talk about making a two- or three-year trip to Mars and back one day, actually have the bodies to back up that boast. That will mean more one-year astronauts, possibly quite a few more.

▲ Above: Kelly shortly after he exited the Soyuz TMA-18M.
▶ Right: crewmates (from left) Mikhail Kornienko, Sergey Volkov and Kelly rest after landing.

"We're looking at as many as 10," says Doug Wheelock, a NASA astronaut and the incoming director of NASA's office at Star City, the Russian space agency's headquarters outside Moscow. "And to get a good data set, we need a good mix of subjects, which means women and men, older crew members and younger ones, veterans and first-timers. There's a lot we have to learn."

That is not cheering news for space partisans missing the golden era of the moon landings, weary of more than 40 years of rowing in circles in low-Earth orbit and anxious to fly off and kick up some Mars dust already. But ambition can't sprint ahead of safety—and there's something to be said for the pokier pace of today compared

with the headlong rush of the moon era.

The space race then may have been fueled by ambition, vision and a commitment to dream up the most difficult, outrageous, improbable thing we could, to give ourselves a deadline—before the end of the 1960s and not a day later!—and then go off and do it. But it was fueled by other, less lovely things too. It was a very big piece of a very cold war, a battle of armies, ideologies and nuclear arms between the U.S. and the now-vanished U.S.S.R., and a flag on the moon for one side was meant as a finger in the eye to the other.

Half a century on, a little ceremony can be held in an airport lounge with room for three flags and three interpreters speaking three different languages. And around them can be men and women in the light-blue jumpsuits of NASA and the dark-blue jumpsuits of Roscosmos, with the American stars and stripes or the Russian tricolor stitched to their shoulders and no one really caring much who was wearing what. Kelly and Kornienko, representatives of those countries, flew together in the same way, and if there will be a medical price to pay for their long year in space, they will pay it together too. But the benefits—as the two of them surely knew before they went, or they wouldn't have gone at all—will belong to our questing, spacefaring species as a whole.

TIME

Editor Nancy Gibbs
Creative Director D.W. Pine
Director of Photography Kira Pollack

A YEAR IN SPACE

Inside Scott Kelly's Historic Mission—Is Travel to Mars Next?

Editors Courtney Mifsud, Eileen Daspin
Writer Jeffrey Kluger
Designer Anne-Michelle Gallero
Photo Editor Heather Casey
Copy Editor Joseph McCombs
Editorial Production David Sloan

A YEAR IN SPACE: THE DOCUMENTARY SERIES

Director Shaul Schwarz
Co-Director Marco Grob
Producer Jonathan D. Woods
Editor Andrey Alistratov
Cinematographers Christina Clusiau, Marco Grob, Shaul Schwarz
Assistant Producer Heather Casey
Executive Producers Mike Beck, Jeffrey Kluger, Ian Orefice, Kira Pollack
Sound Mix Dan Dzula
Title-Sequence Composer Jeremy Turner

TIME INC. BOOKS

Publisher Margot Schupf
Associate Publisher Allison Devlin
Vice President, Finance Terri Lombardi
Vice President, Marketing Jeremy Biloon
Executive Director, Marketing Services Carol Pittard
Director, Brand Marketing Jean Kennedy
Finance Director Kevin Harrington
Assistant General Counsel Andrew Goldberg
Assistant Director, Production Susan Chodakiewicz
Senior Manager, Category Marketing Bryan Christian
Brand Manager Katherine Barnet
Associate Prepress Manager Alex Voznesenskiy
Project Manager Hillary Leary

Editorial Director Stephen Koepp
Creative Director Gary Stewart
Director of Photography Christina Lieberman
Editorial Operations Director Jamie Roth Major
Senior Editor Alyssa Smith
Assistant Art Director Anne-Michelle Gallero
Copy Chief Rina Bander
Assistant Managing Editor Gina Scauzillo
Assistant Editor Courtney Mifsud

Special Thanks NASA, Brad Beatson, Nicole Fisher, Erin Hines, Kristina Jutzi, Seniqua Koger, Kate Roncinske, Krystal Venable

BEHIND THE CAMERAS

A team of TIME journalists and contributors worked for nearly two years to produce the documentary series *A Year in Space*, the basis for an hourlong TIME and PBS feature. The team gathered in Houston in December 2014 with astronaut Scott Kelly (at rear) in a mock-up of the International Space Station, where astronauts train for their missions aboard the ISS. With Kelly, from left in center row, are documentary producer Jonathan Woods, executive producer Jeffrey Kluger and co-director Marco Grob. At front is director Shaul Schwarz. Watch TIME's video series at time.com/space. For information on viewing the full-length documentary, go to pbs.org/yearinspace

CREDITS

COVER Marco Grob *TITLE PAGE* NASA *CONTENTS* NASA *BLASTING INTO THE FUTURE* 4 Marco Grob 7 NASA/Robert Markowitz 8 NASA/Bill Ingalls 10 Martin Gee 11 Marco Grob *LIFTOFF!* 12–13 NASA/Bill Ingalls 14 NASA/Bill Ingalls 15 NASA/Bill Ingalls *THE GREAT TWIN STUDY BEGINS* 16–17 Marco Grob 18 Courtesy of the Kelly Family/NASA 19 Courtesy of the Kelly Family/NASA 20 Marco Grob 21 NASA *AT HOME ABOVE THE WORLD* 22–23 NASA 24–25 NASA (3) *LANDSCAPE MODE* 26–31 NASA/Scott Kelly (3) *GETTING THE WORK DONE* 32–33 NASA 34 NASA 35 NASA (2) 36–37 NASA (3) *LABS AND LEISURE TIME* 38 NASA/Scott Kelly; NASA 39 NASA *THE SPACE SHOT* 40–41 NASA 43 NASA/Regan Geeseman 45 ESA/NASA *WHY SALAD IN SPACE MATTERS* 46 NASA (2) 47 NASA

DOCKING MANEUVERS 48–49 NASA 50 NASA (2) *A RECORD-BREAKING WOMAN* 52–53 ESA/NASA 54 NASA/Bill Ingalls 55 NASA *WATER WORLD* 56–61 NASA/Scott Kelly (6) *SHUTTLING SCIENCE* 62–63 NASA 65 Courtesy Virginia Beach City Public Schools *TIME FOR A WALK* 66–67 NASA (3) *FIFTEEN YEARS AND . . .* 68 NASA 70–71 NASA/Gary Daines; NASA 72 NASA/Charles Babir 73–74 AP Photo/John Raoux; NASA/Scott Kelly; NASA *CITIES FROM ABOVE* 74–79 NASA/Scott Kelly (3) *EMERGENCY SPACE WALK* 80–81 NASA 82–83 NASA (2) *SOCIAL SKILLS* 84–85 NASA/Scott Kelly *THE SEARCH FOR LIFE* 86 NASA, ESA and the Hubble Heritage Team (STScI/AURA) *HOMECOMING* 90–91 NASA/Bill Ingalls 92–93 NASA/Bill Ingalls (3) 94 NASA/Bill Ingalls (2) *BACK COVER* Marco Grob

30798196R00055